TEST YOUR EMOTIONAL INTELLIGENCE

TEST YOUR EMOTIONAL INTELLIGENCE

HOW TO ASSESS AND BOOST YOUR EQ

Robert Wood • Harry Tolley

KOGAN PAGE

London and Sterling, VA

First published in Great Britain and the United States in 2003 by
Kogan Page Limited

120 Pentonville Road   22883 Quicksilver Drive
London N1 9JN   Sterling VA 20166–2012
UK   USA
www.kogan-page.co.uk

ISBN 0 7494 3732 4

British Library Cataloguing in Publication Data
A CIP record for this book is available from the British Library.

Typeset by Saxon Graphics Ltd, Derby
Printed and bound in Great Britain by Clays Ltd, St Ives plc

Contents

Acknowledgements

The references to the American psychologist and writer Daniel Goleman are from his 1999 book *Working with Emotional Intelligence*. The reference to McCabe and Quayle is to an article by Dr Rosemarie McCabe and Dr Ethel Quayle published in *The Psychologist*, January 2002. The UK management practices report mentioned in Chapter 1 and Chapter 6 was issued by Office Angels and was entitled *Managers want the status but would rather not 'manage' others*. It appeared in November 2001. The quotations by Dr Carl Rogers given in Chapter 3 and Chapter 7 are taken from his 1980 book *A Way of Being*. The article quoting Professor Andrew Steptoe was called 'How to handle stress' and appeared in *The Times*, 20 November 2001. The example of Chinese whispers in Chapter 6 was taken from: www.scoutbase.org.uk/activity/games/pages/whispers.

The article describing Dr Clive Sherlock's therapy was called 'Train your mind to fight depression' and described how you can liberate yourself by learning to live with your feelings. It appeared in *The Times* on 16 February 1999. The quotation from Steve Waugh was taken from a piece that appeared in the *Guardian* on 14 February 2002. The reference to Irving Welsh in Chapter 7 comes from an article about him published in *The Times* on 12 April 2002.

Introduction

As experienced observers of human behaviour, we take the considered view that there is every reason for taking emotional intelligence (EI, also referred to as EQ) just as seriously as the mental variety, if not more so. After all, without people perhaps realizing it, evidence on EI has been widely collected in CVs, references, interviews and assessment centre activities as an integral part of recruitment and selection processes. What is new (and hence the relevance of this book) is that attempts are now being made to assess EI more systematically and explicitly by means of tests and inventories designed specifically for the purpose. While not pretending that the measurement is exact (which is also true of other psychometric tests), we are convinced that EI can be sufficiently well assessed that it can provide valuable information on those emotions that drive and shape our day-to-day behaviour.

We assume that as you are a reader of this book, you are interested in obtaining new insights into your own EI, and we have organized its contents in such a way as to help you to achieve that end. The book, therefore, is a mixture of explanatory text that will provide you with an introduction to different aspects of EI, together with test material that will enable you to assess yourself. Chapter 1 presents sample questions that are typical of widely used EI questionnaires and inventories. We then introduce you to the method of assessment that we devised especially for the tests provided in the rest of the book.

In Chapter 7 you are invited to bring together your scores on the different tests that you have done throughout the book, and to use this information as the basis for constructing your own EI profile. The latter can then be used to inform your personal reflection and development planning. The aim is that by the end of the book you will have begun to appreciate how the benefits of assessing and developing your emotional intelligence wash backwards and forwards between your personal life and your relationships, and elsewhere, including your place of work.

What is emotional intelligence?

In this chapter we introduce the notion of emotional intelligence (EI or EQ) and explain how emotions drive our behaviour. We then suggest how EI can be broken down into the following components or competencies: self-awareness; self-regulation; empathy; motivation and social skills. We then provide examples of statements and questions that are typical of those commonly used in EI tests and inventories. Finally, we introduce the method of assessment that has been developed especially for use in the tests provided throughout the rest of the book.

EQ and IQ

When we talk about intelligence we are almost always referring to 'mental' intelligence, or IQ. Like it or not, a whole language has grown up to describe degrees of intelligence. We say of people (although not always to their face since most of these terms are pejorative) that they are 'bright', 'brainy', 'Einstein', 'dim', 'thick', or that they have 'nothing between the ears' – no doubt you could add to the list if asked to do so.

EI (or EQ) has only come into the language in the past 10 years, but colloquialisms for aspects of it have been with us for far longer than that and, indeed, crop up all of the time. For example, how often do we say that someone is a 'loose cannon', or is acting like a 'headless chicken'? Both expressions connote inadequate **self-regulation**. When we say someone is a 'cold fish', we mean that they are over-regulated, lack warmth and therefore **empathy**. But empathy is about more than warmth. For example, if you find yourself saying to someone that they can 'read you like a book', then they are more than likely exhibiting strong empathy. To be cited as a person who is 'together' is a compliment, and signifies a developed **self-awareness**. If you are reckoned to be 'a good mixer', then it is fair to suppose that you have well-developed **social skills**. Finally, it is likely that your **motivation** is being praised if someone says of you that you are 'the early bird [who] catches the worm' or that you 'don't let the grass grow under your feet'.

Ever since it came into prominence in the early 1990s, critics have dismissed the idea of EI as a passing fad. However, those like Daniel Goleman, who have championed the concept of EI, argue that in the workplace possessing mental intelligence is just not enough any more – if it ever was. Let us consider, for example, what is involved in managing people. Plainly, managers in all spheres of work need what is commonly called 'grey matter', not least because they have technical material to absorb, complex problems to solve and difficult decisions to make. But intellect alone is never enough, because many of the problems they encounter are essentially emotional in nature. For example, there are those colleagues who sulk if they don't get their own way, others who can be prickly, throw tantrums, or under-perform for reasons best known to themselves, while others seem to be incapable of working effectively with others.

The ability to handle such people-problems effectively is heavily dependent on being able to manage your own emotional state so that you stay on an even keel, and being in touch with your own inner feelings so that you understand your own drives and preferences. At the same time you need to be able to appreciate other people's points of view and to sense and anticipate how they are likely to respond to any suggestions you might make. Finally, you have to be able to engage with others in a pleasant, mature and considerate way. In short, what is called for is EI of quite a high order.

Goleman is quick to point out that EI is not a 'magic bullet' by which everyone can suddenly become emotionally smart. What he does say is that, where people are involved, anything that serves to bring out the best in others is to be sought after and cultivated. However, a recent survey of UK management practice discovered that not only are many managers found wanting when it comes to communication skills, but a majority of them do not even want to manage people at all.

Despite these findings, our own experience tells us that EI will continue to be at a premium among managers and leaders. It's a tall order, but to be really successful such people need to be self-aware, capable of self-regulation, highly motivated, capable of motivating others, skilled in all aspects of empathy, and possessed of a full range of social skills.

Emotions still drive our behaviour

As any student of the brain will tell you, there is good reason for taking EQ just as seriously as IQ. We know that our emotional impulses are located in a different part of the brain from our rational reflexes. The former were laid down first and are much older than the latter. Thus, when our early ancestors had to respond to physical danger it was through their emotional reflexes. They didn't think first and act later – they acted on impulse.

In some ways it is no different now – but isn't it going out on a limb to say that? We think not. But if you find that assertion difficult to accept, just check it out for yourself by watching any group of people doing a job that is not entirely straightforward and may be beyond their capability. Look out especially for the first time things begin to go wrong. Very quickly you will start to see those telltale signs of agitation, the petulance, the expressed frustration, the snappiness, the hands on hips. In quick succession follow the making of excuses, the giving up and the assignment of blame. Soon the scene is charged with emotion and it isn't long before someone really loses control – 'throws the toys out of the pram' – and storms off.

In reality, our much-vaunted thinking capacities are just a thin veneer that can be easily penetrated or by-passed by our inner feelings. In his novel *Lord of the Flies* William Golding depicts perfectly how in certain circumstances 11-year-old boys can degenerate into savages. Likewise, in a famous experiment (you might have seen the film *The Experiment*) the psychologist Stanley Milgram showed how ordinary people can be made compliant and turned into brutal thugs. In both cases, it was the emotions that were corrupted.

Like it or not, emotions do drive our behaviour – but not necessarily in any coherent or sensible manner. 'Undisciplined squads of emotions', was how it was put by the poet T S Eliot. The challenge facing all of us, therefore, is to decide whether we are going to work with our emotions to help us do what we want to do in life, or to fight them. That has always been the question, but now it is being asked in an environment that is infinitely more complicated than the one inhabited by our early ancestors.

Where our emotions are concerned, are we going to go with the grain, or against it? There is really only one answer. If we go against the grain, wilfully or not, the certain consequence is self-destruction. Emotions have to be reckoned with, which is why the cultivation and nurturing of EI is widely acknowledged as being of such importance. The phrase formulated by the novelist Ernest Hemingway, 'grace under pressure', aptly describes what is needed. It sums up what Hemingway supremely admired in his own heroes – though unfortunately, when the pressures in his life got too much for him, and he could no longer manage with grace, he committed suicide. Such an extreme reaction should serve to remind us that as individuals we all possess a mixture of strengths and weaknesses when it comes to EI. The question is how finely balanced this combination is, and how our lives (and those of others) are affected by it – for better or for worse.

EI defined

It is generally recognized that EI is made up of five components or areas of competence:

- **self-regulation** – being able to manage and control your own emotional state;
- **self-awareness** – knowing yourself and what your emotions are telling you;
- **motivation** – channelling your emotions to enable you to achieve goals;
- **empathy** – recognizing and reading emotions in others;
- **social skills** – relating to and influencing others.

These components are interconnected in complex ways – our ability to perform effectively in any one of them being related to how capable we are in one or more of the others. In other words, there is a root system that runs through all of them. Thus, the handling of feelings in such a way that we behave appropriately (**self-regulation**) is an ability that builds on knowledge of self (**self-awareness**). Likewise, those who are adept at reading their own emotions (**self-awareness**) are likely to be able to read the emotions of other people (**empathy**). The saying 'It takes one to know one' is often used as a put-down, but it is founded on self-awareness and empathy. Being able to relate well to others, sincerely rather than shallowly (**social skills**), is surely a function of all of the others. Similarly, without self-knowledge, that which powers us to achieve – what we call **motivation** – is unlikely to come into play.

When generating the colloquialisms for EI listed above we formed the strong impression that far more of them are associated with failure to self-regulate than with any of the other elements of EI. There is really no end to them – 'lost his rag', 'went ballistic', 'lost it', 'flew off the handle', 'blew a fuse', and so forth. No doubt you can generate some examples of your own!

Such preponderance is pretty much what we would expect. After all, loss of self-control constitutes the most obvious and shocking manifestation of the emotions running riot, whether it is a boxer hitting the referee, a player striking an umpire, or a so-called 'hell-raiser' behaving badly on television. Lack of warmth may be felt strongly at the individual level, but it does not have that same capacity to embarrass; as for absence of self-awareness, being even more private, it may escape notice altogether.

So, self-regulation is a crucial ingredient, but the last thing we would want to do is to give the impression that EI is just about maintenance of self-control, important though that is. If self-regulation is largely (but not wholly) about prevention of gross outbursts that essentially produce negative or even destructive outcomes, then empathy and self-awareness, social skills and motivation are about using the relevant skills constructively in making day-to-day dealings with others more positive, pleasant and productive.

In this book we will introduce you to the five components of EI identified above. In so doing we will illustrate for you the value of excelling and the consequences of falling short on each of these competencies. The idea is that out of these contrasts, and the information to be derived from your performance on the relevant tests, learning points will emerge that can be used in your personal development planning. How far you pursue these learning opportunities is, of course, a matter for you to decide, but if this book helps you to recognize and then break any dysfunctional patterns of behaviour, it will have done its job. Here, now, are the five areas of competence considered in greater detail.

Self-regulation

We have broken down **self-regulation** into the five aspects we see as key. To promote personal development, they are couched in terms of imperatives:

- Defer judgement; curb impulse.
- Park the problem; detach yourself.

- Express yourself, but do it assertively, not aggressively.
- Be flexible; go with the flow; don't force things.
- Manage your non-verbal communication.

If and when you seek to assess your EQ through the various commercial products on the market, you will meet statements like the ones we are going to introduce next. Try responding to them as you go along and in so doing you should begin to gain some insights into your own EI.

The first set of statements is intended to assess aspects of your self-control (or lack of it). Try to be honest in your answers; otherwise the only person you are deceiving is yourself. That applies to all the tests in this book, especially to the ones provided in Chapters 2–6, which are intended to provide you with a means of auditing your EI and building up your own EQ profile (Chapter 7). To help you get the idea, take a look at the item given below. Notice that is consists of a statement ('I'm impatient') to which there are five possible responses. All you have to do is to put a tick in the box that most accurately describes your behaviour.

Statement	Always	Mostly	Sometimes	Rarely	Never
I'm impatient					

To our mind this is a good EI test statement – direct, unambiguous and, since we are talking about self-control, very much to the point. You must know if you are impatient or not – in other words whether your choice is 'Always' or 'Mostly'. Now respond to the following statement by putting a tick in the appropriate box.

Statement	Always	Mostly	Sometimes	Rarely	Never
I find it hard to control my anger					

This is another good direct statement because you should know if you have a problem controlling your anger – hence you should have had no difficulty at locating yourself on the five-point scale. Now that you are getting the idea, try the next one.

Statement	Always	Mostly	Sometimes	Rarely	Never
I like to get things off my chest					

If you answer this one as 'Always' or 'Mostly', you are saying that your self-restraint is fragile, and that you are rather unwilling to keep things to yourself. Now try the next statement.

Statement	Always	Mostly	Sometimes	Rarely	Never
I like to make my position clear					

Clearly, the above item is intended to find out where you fit on an assertiveness scale. Having decided upon your response, you might give some thought as to what it tells you about yourself – especially if you response was 'Always' or 'Never'. Now see how you respond to the following item.

Statement	Always	Mostly	Sometimes	Rarely	Never
I like to have the last word					

Notice that there is a more belligerent tone to this statement. If you respond 'Always' or 'Mostly', you are signalling not only that you will not back down in an argument or discussion, but that you are also likely to be inflexible.

Now that you are into the way of working, here are some more statements probing aspects of your self-control. As before, respond by putting ticks in the appropriate boxes.

Statement	Always	Mostly	Sometimes	Rarely	Never
If someone has a go at me, I go quiet					
In a group I find I badly want to speak but can't					
I blurt things out					
I like to speak my mind					
I like the sound of my own voice					
When I begin to feel hot and bothered I mentally count to 10					
If I see or hear people arguing, I get agitated					

After all that, you should now be ready to tackle another type of statement, which can be used to assess either yourself or some other person. Such statements are cast in a format suitable for use in what is known as '360-degree evaluation'. This means that as many people as you like can evaluate you (referred to as 'this person' in the statements given below), in addition to yourself. Record your response by putting a tick in the appropriate box beside each statement.

Statement	Always	Mostly	Sometimes	Rarely	Never
Put under pressure (this person) cracks					
(This person) is able to carry on in the face of setbacks					
(This person) over-reacts to trivial issues					
(This person) likes to go his or her own way					
(This person) uses his or her presence to intimidate					

Self-awareness

We have broken down **self-awareness** into those aspects we see as key to EI behaviour, and expressed them as imperatives:

- Respect yourself.
- Be positive.
- Be true to yourself.
- Give logic and rationality a rest.
- Listen to others.
- Understand your impact on others.

Now for some sample statements that are intended to test your self-awareness. They are typical of those you will come across in published EI tests and inventories. Notice that they have the same format as the items you have already worked through, and should be answered in exactly the same way.

Statement	Always	Mostly	Sometimes	Rarely	Never
I'm in touch with my emotions					

The problem with this statement is that it finesses the issue of what self-awareness is in the first place. It's easy to say you are in touch with your feelings (or hard to say you are not in touch), but the matter needs more exploration. So have a go at the next item.

Statement	Always	Mostly	Sometimes	Rarely	Never
It's hard for me to accept myself just as I am					

With this item, if you answer 'Always' or 'Mostly' you are saying that you are inclined to be self-critical – perhaps more often than is healthy for you. Would the opposite be true if you answered 'Never' or 'Rarely'? Now try the next statement.

Statement	Always	Mostly	Sometimes	Rarely	Never
If I have to describe my feelings, I get flustered					

This item goes towards the heart of the matter with regard to self-awareness. Answer 'Always' or 'Mostly' and you are saying that you are largely incapable of talking in terms of feelings – yours or anyone else's – and that you would rather not have to do it at all. See how you respond to the next item.

Statement	Always	Mostly	Sometimes	Rarely	Never
I feel awkward if I have to kiss people outside my family					

Again, an answer of 'Always' or 'Mostly' signifies some degree of emotional inhibition on your part. What about the next statement?

Statement	Always	Mostly	Sometimes	Rarely	Never
If something isn't right for me then I won't do it					

You have to be really high in EI to answer 'Always' to this one. Most of us end up doing the wrong thing from our own point of view for at least some of the time – even though some of us realize that we have not chosen the right option. The main thing is to build on that realization, learn from any negative experiences, and do your best to avoid them in future. Now move on to the next item.

Statement	Always	Mostly	Sometimes	Rarely	Never
My preference is for factual rather than fictional films and books					

If your answer was 'Always', the inference is that you prefer to keep irrationality and playfulness at arm's length. On the other hand, if your response was 'Never', your preferences would seem to lie in the direction of escapism. Here now are a few questions for you to tackle written in the 360-degree style.

Statement	Always	Mostly	Sometimes	Rarely	Never
(This person) is prejudiced					

Prejudice is an aspect of negativity, which this item deals with squarely – as does the next statement.

Statement	Always	Mostly	Sometimes	Rarely	Never
(This person) complains that things are difficult					

To moan or complain all the time is, of course, another form of negativity and one that is likely to have a detrimental effect on both you and other people. A less pessimistic response is to see difficulties as challenges – an important aspect of motivation, as will now be revealed.

Motivation

We have sub-divided **motivation** into four key aspects:

- striving to improve and to achieve high standards;
- being committed to achieving your goals;
- taking the initiative and seizing opportunities;
- being optimistic even in the face of adversity.

Here are some statements that will help you to begin to explore aspects of your motivation. They are typical of those you will come across in published inventories and you should respond to them in the same way as previous items.

Statement	Always	Mostly	Sometimes	Rarely	Never
When there is something unpleasant to be done, I do it right away and get it over with					
When there is something unpleasant to be done, I wait until I have no choice but to do it					
When there is something unpleasant to be done, I find someone to do it for me					

These three items are obviously variations on a theme and you might come up against all three. If you answer 'Always' or even 'Mostly' to each of them, you are conveying a sense that whatever you do is done grudgingly, and is therefore unlikely to represent your best work. True, getting someone else to do things for you might produce acceptable outcomes, but how are you going to feel about it? Will you derive any 'job satisfaction' from it? Will you take all the credit or will you give 'credit where credit is due'? You should also bear in mind that there is a limit to how many times people will tolerate such behaviour. Here are some more statements for you to consider.

Statement	Always	Mostly	Sometimes	Rarely	Never
I'm prepared to go the extra mile					
I won't stop until the job is done properly					
I get stuck in					
I let things get me down					
I find a way round obstacles					
If I can cut corners, I do					
If you can cut corners, you should					

Notice that the last two items raise significantly different issues from each other. In the penultimate statement, a propensity to cut corners could be said to indicate that you have a less than perfect devotion to achievement. The final item raises another issue: it is one thing to say that you are willing to cut corners, quite another to urge it on others. That comes very close to knowing what is best for others as well as for you, and as such it is not an emotionally intelligent way of behaving. Now see what you make of the next item, in which the responses you are offered differ from those used in the preceding items. Record your answer in the same way as before.

Statement	True	Partly true	Not really true	Untrue
(This person) could sell sand in the Sahara				

The enterprising behaviour referred to in this statement is something that is easily recognized by others – so this item would be very suitable for use in 360-degree type inventories.

Empathy

We have broken down **empathy** into four key aspects:

- being sensitive towards and understanding other people;
- making the needs and interests of others your point of reference;
- furthering the development of other people;
- being socially and politically tuned in.

The statements below are intended to test your empathy. They are typical of those you will come across in published inventories.

Statement	Always	Mostly	Sometimes	Rarely	Never
I care what happens to other people					

No doubt you found this item pretty straightforward – after all, you should know whether you care for other people or not. But bear in mind that 'sympathy' is not 'empathy'. It is one thing to write a condolences card or commiserate with someone over a misfortune. It is another matter to feel genuinely what the other person must be going through and, if appropriate, to offer help and support in the light of that knowledge. When Princess Diana died, how many of us poured out sympathy for the bereaved in a generalized, unfocused kind of way and how many empathized with those same people? Or, in being so maudlin, were we just feeling sorry for ourselves? Self-pity is not an emotionally intelligent form of behaviour. Now take a look at the next item.

Statement	Always	Mostly	Sometimes	Rarely	Never
People don't have to tell me what they are feeling – I can sense it					

The problem with this statement is its transparency. It is an open invitation to agree that empathizing comes naturally to you. You might believe that this statement is a true description of your behaviour, but in all probability your claim needs closer examination. One way to go about making such an examination is to cross-check your response with what other people think about you in this respect. The opportunity for such 'triangulation' is one of the benefits of 360-degree evaluation. Now try responding to the following statement.

Statement	Always	Mostly	Sometimes	Rarely	Never
I'm a team player					

Most people will know immediately whether or not they are a team player. But remember you can overplay this role – you can submerge your individuality too much in the interests of the group or team. Of course, that is not a position that would be recognized in societies where emerging as an individual from the rest is neither expected nor encouraged. Now take a look at the next statement.

Statement	Always	Mostly	Sometimes	Rarely	Never
I work hard for other people					

Presumably, if you are a nurse, doctor or teacher – one of the so-called 'caring professions' – this will have been reflected in your response to this item. Here are some more statements for you to think about on aspects of your empathy using the 360-degree format.

Statement	True	Partly true	Not really true	Untrue
People can turn to (this person) in a jam				
(This person) can suss out what is going on				
(This person) likes to help younger people				
(This person) is self-centred				

Social skills

We have sub-divided **social skills** into the three key aspects:

- developing and sustaining interpersonal relationships;
- communicating with others;
- working with others.

Here are some statements with which you can begin to explore the testing of your social skills. As with the examples you have already encountered, they are typical of those you will come across in published EI inventories. When you have completed your responses to each item, give some thought to what they seem to be telling you (individually and collectively) about this aspect of your EI.

Statement	Always	Mostly	Sometimes	Rarely	Never
I get tense when I meet people					
I can talk to anybody					
I am able to deal with difficult 'phone calls					
When a problem arises and nobody seems to know what to do I am able to take charge of the situation					
I make a positive impact on first meeting					
I am fun to be with					
I make you feel comfortable					

Assessment

This section covers the approach to assessment we have adopted for the purposes of this book.

By now, having worked through some sample test items, you should have begun to form an impression of the state of your EI. By working systematically through the rest of this book, including the tests at the end of each chapter, you will deepen and consolidate that self-knowledge. As you will see from what comes next, we favour a rather different approach to assessment from the examples we have used thus far. This will become apparent to you as you work your way through the rest of this chapter in preparation for the test material provided in Chapters 2–6.

Essentially, what we are trying to do is to help you to establish where you are located on a continuum of emotionally intelligent behaviour. To heighten reality, we have framed all of the questions in terms of problems that arise in real-world situations. Although you may find that you have never been in exactly the same situation in every case, you should be able to imagine what it would have been like if you had from your experiences in similar circumstances.

As you work your way through the various tests, you will find that in each item there are always three possible answers: A, B or C. In each case one of the three has been designed to represent the most emotionally intelligent response; another has been written to represent the least emotionally intelligent response; and the third to depict an intermediate position between the two extremes.

It is unlikely that you will have a full quota of most emotionally intelligent answers on any of the tests, unless of course you are that exceptional human being, the person who has real EI – in which case, congratulations. However, if you do respond honestly to each item, and in so doing your end result includes a large number of those responses, we suggest that you check your self-evaluations against those of someone who knows you well and whose judgements you trust. As for the least emotionally intelligent answers, you can perhaps draw your own conclusions from how many you award yourself. But, once again, if you find that you have scored a lot of these, please triangulate your judgements about yourself with assessments made by someone who knows you very well. After all, it is possible that you have been too self-critical, which is not an emotionally intelligent thing to do, as you will see from Chapter 3.

Sometimes you will feel that you could have chosen two of the three responses. If so, try to choose the one that represents your truest and deepest response. Here, then, are some examples of the test items you will meet in subsequent chapters of the book. In each case answer by circling A, B or C – the option that is closest to what you would do, or have been doing, in such a situation.

Someone challenges something you say. How do you respond?
A. Say, 'That's just the sort of thing I'd expect from you'.
B. Ask the person, 'What's wrong with my point of view'?
C. Say, 'I have another opinion, but I'd like to hear what others have to say first'.

This question assesses the 'keep an open mind' aspect of self-regulation. Answer C represents the most emotionally intelligent response because the challenge is not taken personally, and it seeks to open up the discussion to contributions from other people while at the same time indicating that the respondent still has other opinions to express. In contrast, option A is the least emotionally intelligent because the response takes the form of an attack on the person responsible for the challenge, thus provoking a 'slanging match' rather than an orderly exchange of ideas.

You need a report urgently. What do you say to the person responsible for producing it?
A. 'I need you to submit your report to me today.'
B. 'We need that report today.'
C. 'The report is needed today.'

This question assesses the assertive aspect of self-regulation. The preferred answer is A because it signifies a willingness to deal personally with the issue and not hide behind 'we' or an impersonal imperative like answer C. As for answer B, at least the use of 'we' asserts some personal connection and shared responsibility.

You show a friend some holiday snaps and he or she says complimentary things about the way you look. How do you respond?
A. Say, 'You must be joking. I need to lose three stone – minimum. Look at those chins, yuk.'
B. Say, 'Thanks, I felt really good all holiday.'
C. Say, 'Yes, they're not bad. The sun can be kind.'

This question assesses the 'don't be down on yourself' aspect of **self-awareness**. Answering A is more or less equivalent to answering 'Always' to the earlier statement 'It's hard for me to accept myself just as I am'. Answer C smacks a little of putting yourself down, but is better than A, whereas answer B displays a healthy self-regard.

You are away on a course with a few colleagues. During a break you ring into the office to find out if you have any messages. What do you do during that call?
A. Find out what messages you have, if any, and how so-and-so in the office is doing.
B. Find out what messages you have, if any, how so-and-so is doing, and also whether there are any messages for your colleagues.
C. Find out what messages you have, if any.

This question assesses the self-centred aspect of **empathy**. Self-centred people are only interested in looking out for themselves. Anyone who answers C has the right intentions, but is not thinking of the people he or she is actually with on the course. Acting with reciprocity towards colleagues and friends – 'do as you would be done by' – is what makes social life go round. In that respect, B is the most emotionally intelligent answer of the three.

You are in a group working on an important task against a tight deadline. A colleague is constantly distracting you by 'horsing around'. How do you respond?
A. Signal that you have lost patience by telling the person to 'shut up and grow up'.
B. Suggest that the group does a progress review and generates ideas for meeting the deadline.
C. Ignore the behaviour, do your best to concentrate on the task in hand, and remind the group of the impending deadline.

This question assesses the 'striving to achieve high standards' aspect of **motivation**. Answer A is self-centred, puts the blame for the lack of progress on one individual and runs the risk of alienating the rest of the group. Answer C is better because it indicates a desire to meet the deadline, though all that it really does is nag the group, which may or may not have a beneficial effect. Thus, answer B is the most emotionally intelligent response because it tries to find a process for focusing the efforts of the group (including the person causing the problem) on the task in hand.

You have to field a call from an angry customer about a defective product. How do you respond?
A. Argue with the customer about what exactly is wrong, and ask why, if the product is so bad, the company has not been inundated with other complaints.
B. Point out that if products go wrong it is usually because of the way they have been handled or stored, but that a refund or exchange will be possible.
C. Say that you will exchange the product or refund the price, but ask the customer to explain under what circumstances the product went wrong.

This question assesses the communications aspect of **social skills** in an area – customer service – where EI should be at a premium. It should be easy to see, therefore, why answer A is the least emotionally intelligent response, and C the most acceptable.

You realize that you have made a wrong decision, which will have an adverse effect on other people. How do you respond?
A. Try to think of ways of limiting the damage you have caused.
B. Keep quiet about it, and in the meantime look for somebody else to take the blame.
C. Apologize to the people concerned, and put forward some proposals for repairing the damage.

This question assesses the 'working with others' aspect of **social skills**. In terms of working with EI, if you make mess of things, the best thing you can do is accept the responsibility and seek ways of making good the damage you have caused (answer C) rather than trying to shift the blame on to the people with whom you work (answer B). The chances are that attempts at damage limitation (answer A) will make matters worse rather than better.

In the rest of the book

In Chapters 2–6 you will be presented with a series of tests made up of questions of the type you have just seen. At the end of each chapter you are invited to make a note of your test scores in order to see where you stand on the relevant component of EI. Finally, in Chapter 7 we will explain how to pull together all of your scores to produce your own EQ profile.

2

Self-regulation

The song says, 'I've got to give vent to my emotions', but it does not mean that you have to follow suit. After all, what is being urged is pretty strong stuff. 'Vent' is what volcanoes do, and 'got to' is – well – 'got to'. Granted, we are quite fond of using volcanic imagery to describe how Mr or Ms Angry: 'erupted', 'blew his or her top' or was 'sulphurous', 'seismic' or 'fuming'. But volcanoes are inanimate, driven by physical forces and can't help but erupt, while we are human and we can help it – for us there is the possibility of self-regulation.

Management and control of emotions

Self-regulation is about being able to manage and control your emotional states, the key words being 'manage' and 'control'. The song quoted above continues, 'I'm only content having my way'. Clive Sherlock, a consultant psychiatrist in Oxford, has something to say about that: 'If we learn to tolerate a feeling then something changes. It is not grinning and bearing it. It is being willing to let go of the thought 'I must have my own way'.

What does he mean by this? Suppose you have been reluctant to accept a relative by marriage, preferring out of dislike to ignore that person. Now, through regard for your blood relative and possibly after an appeal by him or her, you decide that in future you will embrace the spouse. If henceforth you act sincerely in accordance with your resolve then you are doing much more than 'grinning and bearing it'. Moreover, by abandoning your hostility to the person in question you have given up having your own way, which was to blank out that person from your life.

There are other sentiments in the lyric that appeal to many of us. It is, after all, a celebration of the free spirit – 'there is no other life of which I'm fonder' and 'if I am fancy free, and love to wander, it's just the gypsy in my soul'. That sounds pretty good: the snag is that we have to live alongside each other, and that means exercising responsibility and some regard for the next person. A world where we all decided that we would do exactly what we wanted, when we wanted, with whom we wanted, and to hell with the consequences, would be impossibly hedonistic. Some self-regulation in society – actually, quite a lot – is necessary for it to function effectively.

The knack of self-regulation lies in working with your feelings, not giving in to them. Feelings are not tyrants to be appeased routinely, although it can seem that way. There are ways to resist. Instead of thinking, 'I must have it now' or 'I must get this off my chest', try thinking, 'Do I really want it now?' or 'Do I really want it?' or 'What is the price of having it now?' By delaying gratification and stifling impulsiveness, you achieve control over yourself and immediately put yourself at an advantage over all those others whose instinct is to indulge themselves instantly.

Do I really want it?

Think of something you have been wanting, or something you wanted and got. Do you (or did you) really want it? Would it matter (or would it have mattered) if you don't (or didn't) get it? Could you wait (or have waited) for it?

By the way, in case you wondered, the answers do not have to be 'No'. We are not in the business of denying pleasure, just asking questions.

Self-regulation is about managing feelings so that you behave in a manner that is appropriate for the circumstances. If you have experienced a setback of some kind, it is about being able to find a perspective that enables you to shake off irritability, gloom or immobilizing anxiety. People who are lacking in this ability are forever battling with feelings of distress, and dwelling on things by refusing to 'let things lie'. So-called soap operas on television are full of such people, but that is the point, of course. You don't manage your feelings in a television drama; you just let them 'hang out' for everyone to see. In contrast, there are those who are able to bounce back quickly from whatever life throws at them. Politicians and top sporting personalities are good at this, and have to be. You will often hear them calmly say, 'It's happened. There's nothing I can do about it; let's move on.'

Behaviour at work, and outside work, is usually different – sometimes very different. Because we are working alongside others, exercising self-control at work is bound to be a more focused affair. It means being able to handle emotions so that they facilitate rather than interfere with the task at hand. It involves acting conscientiously, with integrity, and taking responsibility for your personal performance – there is no room for behaving like a prima donna or 'throwing a wobbly'.

Attitude

Think of some people you know who are obviously performing below their potential. What do you see them doing? Why do you think they are behaving this way? Is there anything you feel like saying to them that might help them?

What ideas did you generate from this exercise? Perhaps you came up with some of these: lack of consideration; blaming others; complaining about other people; 'bad-mouthing' the organization; openly criticizing others, especially bosses; being late; leaving early; being argumentative; picking fights; refusing to give respect to others; pushing rules to the limit; grumbling about pay, and so on.

We suggest that many of these behaviours fall squarely into the category of what is usefully called 'attitude'. People with attitude are often at war with themselves or their feelings are out of kilter – they are 'emotionally disconnected'. Typically, they believe that they are being overlooked unfairly, that no one understands them and that they are the only ones 'in step'. As often as not, these are the people who bring their personal difficulties with them to work, and they allow those problems to distract themselves and others from the tasks they are paid to perform.

'Don't bottle it up', you hear it said. 'Get it out, don't let it fester.' A whole range of medical problems, including the incidence of cancer, has even been attributed to 'not letting it out'. So surely it must be good – unconditionally – to express your emotions? The answer, as so often, is 'yes and no'. The basic rule is: if you are going to let it out, make sure you do something constructive with it. If it is only going to have an adverse effect on you, then forget it. In professional tennis there are players who seem to engineer emotional outbursts in their matches in order to use them to their advantage. 'You cannot be serious!' is what one great US player once shouted to a Wimbledon umpire. On the other hand, some players let their emotions get out of control and end up 'losing it' – in both senses.

Self-regulation is about not 'losing it'. It is easy to tell when this is happening to you because you experience the rather unpleasant sensation of becoming upset and losing control over yourself. You don't know what you are going to blurt out, or what you are going to do with your face or your limbs. Once this happens, you haven't got a chance of accomplishing what you were seeking to achieve, because all of your energies are now directed inwards to deal with your own emotions as well as the consequences of your actions.

Lost it recently?

Think of a time in your own life when you 'lost it'. You wanted to make a point but became so overcome by strong feelings of anger or injustice that you flooded with emotion, lost the thread, if not the plot, and had to retreat or, worse, crawl away, still seething.

Now think of an instance of a similar kind where you managed to control your inner feelings. What was the difference? Did you concentrate harder the second time? Did you prepare better? Had you written something down?

Did you ask yourself, 'What's the worst thing that could happen if I share my thoughts in a civil, clear-headed manner?' Because if you do ask yourself that question, you will find that the worst thing that could happen is not very awful at all. Perhaps you will be ignored or your ideas rejected, but at least you will have made your point as well as retaining your composure.

Too much self-regulation

Could there be a downside to regulating your emotions? Mightn't control degenerate into over-control? We all know of individuals who cannot or will not express their inner feelings. We often give them labels like 'uptight', 'cold fish', 'ice maiden', 'wooden' or say they have a 'stiff upper lip', while the US writer Dorothy Parker said of such a person 'she ran the gamut of emotions from A to B'.

It is easy to poke fun at such people, but then the same applies to the overtly tearful – like some recent Oscar winners. It seems to us that as a general rule, keeping your emotions under control, frustrating and tiresome though it may be for you and for others, is almost certainly a better option. It is certainly a more emotionally intelligent way of coping than exposing your inner feelings to all and sundry. If you make a habit of letting people know exactly how you are feeling all of the time, the danger is that you become too transparent and easy to read. Your behaviour, therefore, becomes predictable, which in turn can leave you open to manipulation by means of 'emotional blackmail'.

There is such a thing as being too emotional in your dealings with others – 'no need to give a penny for their thoughts'. By all means wear your 'heart on your sleeve' when it is appropriate to do so, like when you feel really passionate about something. However, you need to avoid investing your routine interactions (such as with friends and colleagues at work) with an excess of emotion.

In summary, self-regulation is about striking a balance. There is definitely a golden mean to be sought between over- and under-regulation, but in our view it should be located closer to over- than to under-regulation. To that end, by the time you have worked your way through the rest of this chapter, we would expect you to have:

- a clear understanding of what it is to regulate your behaviour;
- a knowledge of how well you do it;
- some ideas on what you can do to extend and enhance those things you already do well.

Aspects of self-regulation

You will recall that in Chapter 1 we broke self-regulation down into the five aspects that we see as being of key importance:

- Defer judgement; curb impulses.
- Park the problem; detach yourself.
- Express yourself, but do it assertively, not aggressively.
- Be flexible; go with the flow; don't force things.
- Manage your non-verbal communication.

We will now discuss these in more detail. You will find a short test associated with each one at the end of the chapter. You can do the tests one at a time as you work your way through the text, or do all the tests at the end after you have read the whole chapter – the choice is yours. When you come to do the tests, you will notice that some of the questions that appear in different tests look to be similar to each other. This is a reflection of the degree of overlap there is between different aspects of the same competency – a point you will come to appreciate as you read through the book. Nevertheless, the outcomes from the tests should provide you with appropriate measures of your emotional intelligence.

Defer judgement: curb impulses

The more judgemental you are, the more things you find to get angry about. For example, if you allow yourself to get irritated by white vans, boy racers, flash cars, foreign cars, old cars, new cars, dirty cars, cars with one headlight, coaches that hog the middle lane, trucks that pull out in front of you, then 'road rage' is not far away. It certainly makes for an easier life (refer to 'Respect yourself' in Chapter 3) if you suspend judgement – not all of the time, because occasionally you need or are required to make a quick, even a snap, judgement, but most of the time.

The same applies to curbing impulses; taking the advice 'count to 10' (or even 100) really is a good idea. So why not take the time to examine specific examples of your impulsive behaviour and, in so doing, reflect on how they turned out for you and for other people? You may well find that many impulsive acts were so trivial that they hardly mattered – it's often the big decisions made on impulse that prove costly. For example, considering the outlay, why is it that so many people spend so little time looking round the house they end up buying, or researching the area in which it is located? To move to the seaside on the strength of a holiday there in the summer only to find that it is too cold and quiet in winter is a costly mistake. Similarly, to make a major purchase, such as buying a car, purely on impulse is to run the risk of bitter disappointment. The advice would seem to be: beware of your unfettered impulses!

That said, you must not, as we say elsewhere ('Respect yourself', Chapter 3), be too hard on yourself. Impulses can give us some of the happiest moments of our lives if we get them right. For example, some friends call round unexpectedly with a present, which they say is in celebration of many years of friendship. In response, and without thinking, you open up that bottle you've been saving for a special occasion. A pleasant evening ensues – an example of the good side of impulsive behaviour. The trouble begins, however, when you make a habit of acting on impulse and taking most of your decisions in that way.

Park the problem; detach yourself

When people become agitated they are often told to 'let it go' – to detach themselves from whatever is causing them so much grief. In effect, they are being advised to 'park the problem' so that they can return to it, if they have to, when their emotions have calmed down and they are in a better frame of mind. The person upstairs keeps you awake by playing loud music deep into the night, or a neighbour refuses to cut a hedge that is blocking out the light. What starts as a minor irritation can become an obsession causing you to get 'uptight'. Is there an emotionally intelligent response to such a situation and, if so, what is it?

What we need to do is to try to leave the source of irritation alone for some time before returning to it, preferably armed with a fresh perspective on the problem. Of course that is easier said than done, and you cannot leave problems alone entirely, because nothing may ever happen to resolve them. That is why in some situations it is important that, without overreacting, you voice your complaint, and let it be known how strongly you feel about the matter. But you should also realize that in time what is bothering you may well correct itself without further action on your part. Indeed, you might not have to wait too long before it happens – every river eventually runs into the sea! This realization can induce a sense of inner calm – a state that can be called 'cool optimism'. For anyone who is inclined to become agitated, this state of being is well worth striving for.

Support for this idea comes from the psychologist Andrew Steptoe, who talks not about parking problems, but about what amounts to the same thing: stepping back from your emotional responses. He says:

> A lot of stress comes from the way you lead your life – the amount you're trying to do in a certain time, the way you look at problems, and getting wound up about things which, from the outside, don't look that important... So, learning to prioritize rather than doing everything at once is an important part of managing one's life.

Are you prioritizing?

Take a look at your life and the things with which you are trying to cope. Are you prioritizing or simply attempting to do everything at once? If the latter, are you aware of being under stress? Are there some issues you could park for a while? Is there a problem from which you could afford to detach yourself?

Take a few minutes to see what you can do to rearrange commitments in your life.

If you think about it (and it is a paradox that we have to think so hard about our emotions), it is often because we are trying to do too many things at once that we become agitated, stressed and impulsive. So, if we take the time to think about and prioritize our commitments, inevitably some will be relegated to the back of the queue, and some might even be discarded altogether. It then follows that if we judge certain matters to be relatively unimportant, why should we take them so seriously that we allow them to have an adverse impact on our emotions? 'Get your priorities right' and 'keep a sense of proportion' are two pieces of advice to which you might give further thought in relation to this aspect of self-regulation.

Express yourself, but do it assertively, not aggressively

If you would like to say something in conversation or at a meeting, but feel so shy and self-conscious that you just clam up, then you are not managing and controlling your emotions. If you find yourself in situations like this, you need to find ways of regulating your inner feelings in order to change your behaviour. One option open to you is to steel yourself to be more assertive by not giving in to those feelings of shyness and self-consciousness. The danger of course is that in your determination to be assertive your behaviour tips over into aggression, or you retreat back into your shell because you have allowed your feelings to get the better of you, and end up not expressing yourself once again.

It is important, therefore, to distinguish between assertive and aggressive forms of behaviour. You are behaving assertively when you express your thoughts, feelings and beliefs in direct, honest ways that do not violate another person's integrity. Assertion involves showing respect for both your own needs and feelings and for those of other people. By contrast, you are behaving aggressively when you express your thoughts, feelings and beliefs in ways that humiliate, degrade, belittle or overpower other people. A common and particularly cowardly form of aggression, where the desire to humiliate is obvious, is throwing out some hurtful remark or aside with no regard for its consequences. In other words, aggression is where little or no respect is shown for thoughts and feelings other than your own – behaviour that shows a lack of both self-regulation and empathy (see Chapter 5).

Of course, you can opt to continue to behave non-assertively by failing to express your feelings, thoughts and beliefs directly and honestly, or expressing them in such an understated way that it is easy for others to ignore them. However, it follows – and we cannot emphasize this enough – that non-assertive behaviour is just as indicative as aggressive behaviour of feelings that are not being properly regulated. It is not an emotionally intelligent response.

So why doesn't everybody behave assertively? Typically, people cite fear of reprisals from people in authority, a desire not to 'rock the boat', aiming to please others, low self-esteem and lack of confidence as reasons why they are not assertive. It is certainly true that it takes a lot of determination to complain in public for the first time about poor service you have received, or to challenge the views of someone in authority, but once you have learnt to express yourself in this way, the habit catches on quickly, and it can be rather liberating. Why should you muzzle yourself and accept second-rate treatment or opinions? So, say your piece, but do it calmly and courteously. You will feel emotionally better and stronger for having done it.

Be flexible; go with the flow; don't force things

Just as a rigid object snaps more easily than a supple one, so clinging to fixed views, or persevering with typical behaviour irrespective of what others are doing, is liable to lead to emotional distress – not just for you but for others. If you happen to be with a group that is enjoying itself without people competing against each other – say on a walking trip or a cycle ride – why be the one who competes? It will certainly get you noticed, but not necessarily for the right reasons. Before long others start comparing notes and you can soon become the object of unfriendly remarks, which can cause distress – unless of course you are so insensitive that you can be said to have a 'thick skin'.

Sometimes there are situations in which it is impossible for you to achieve your goals, and for your own emotional well-being it may be in your best interests to recognize that fact and accept it. At times, forcing the issue just doesn't make sense, because the more you try, the more frustrated you become – you are 'beating your head against a brick wall'. An emotionally intelligent response to such a situation would be to re-examine your goals and the means by which you are seeking to achieve them. As you will discover when you find out more about motivation (see Chapter 4), redoubling your efforts may not be the best way forward; there are 'many ways of skinning a rabbit', so changing the way you are doing things may be the better option.

You should also remember to try to keep a sense of proportion at all times. There are many points of decisions in our daily lives where so little hangs on the outcome that it is really not worth getting into a lather about it if the decision doesn't go exactly the way you would have preferred. Here are some examples: Should we eat meat or fish tonight? Should we turn left or right? Should we have our eggs boiled or poached? Who cares? Probably you, if you are the kind of person who has to have a view on anything and everything, and who gets frustrated and angry if you don't get your own way all the time. If you are such an individual, try being a bit more 'easy-going'. If you do, you'll find that it cuts down on the emotional wear and tear. So, you might want to reflect on the merits of 'going with the flow' if you are the kind of person who is willing to 'cut off your nose to spite your face'.

Manage your non-verbal communication

Body language is so informative that it is often our non-verbal communication that sends out signals about the true state of our inner emotions. Whether it is staring out of the window, fidgeting, fiddling, shuffling, doodling, scanning the watch, looking at the clock, leaning back – it will say something to those observing your behaviour. Though much would depend on the context, the chances are that they would interpret aspects of your behaviour as a manifestation of boredom, anxiety or an inability to concentrate.

So the message is that, whether we like it or not, people are going to judge our inner emotions by body language – correctly or otherwise. Consequently, we need to give careful thought not just to what we are saying, but to the accompanying non-verbal messages we are sending out about our feelings. If we don't exercise such care, we are likely to use body language that is inappropriate. For example, excessive finger wagging, head nodding and hand chopping can easily be interpreted as a manifestation of aggression. Secondly, these mannerisms can be so obtrusive that they detract from the verbal message – or indeed obliterate it altogether. There used to be a popular science presenter on television whose body language was so outrageous that, despite all the interesting things he had to say, all that you could ever remember was what he did with his hands.

Not all non-verbal language is disrespectful or counter-productive. Non-verbal language can be used most constructively to augment what is said. Indeed, we may soon stop referring to non-verbal language as such and talk instead about integrated auditory and visual communication. One of us is aware (see Chapter 3) that he is operating in such a fashion when talking to a Dutch colleague. He is conscious of reinforcing what he says with quite forceful gestures and use of the head. Although it is probably quite unnecessary, given how well the colleague speaks English, the purpose is to minimize misunderstanding. However, you need to be aware that there are subtle differences in the ways in which people from other cultures use and read body language. Consequently, in order to reduce misunderstanding in cross-cultural communication (see Chapter 6) care has to be taken to regulate the use of body language.

Watch your body language

Unless you use a video recorder, it is in fact difficult to actually 'watch' your own body language – but what the title to this exercise highlights is the importance of taking care to regulate its use. The first step in doing that is to try to become more aware of when and how you, and other people, use different kinds of non-verbal communication. To that end, study the list below and add further examples that come to mind. Then think about the contexts in which you use them, or have observed them being employed by others. Were they being used appropriately or inappropriately in your view? How did you arrive at these conclusions? Are there ways in which you could improve your use of body language, in terms of the following:

- wagging the finger;
- folding the arms when face to face with others;
- cupping the hands behind the head;
- fidgeting;
- yawning – stifled and unstifled;
- using invasive or flamboyant hand movements;
- head pecking;
- leaning back;
- putting your feet on the desk;
- fiddling with paper clips or pens or hair or spectacles – or anything;
- chewing gum;
- doodling or scribbling notes to others;
- other activities (add your own)?

The tests

For every **item** in each of the **tests** choose **one** answer by circling option A, B or C. Remember, in the cause of accuracy of assessment, you should circle the action closest to what you would do, or have been doing. Do not opt for what you now think is the best or most admirable thing to do. After all, to want to put yourself in the most favourable light is hardly an emotionally intelligent way of responding. A key is provided at the end of the tests, which will enable you to score your answers.

Test 1

1. You see an item in a mail order catalogue or on a Web site that you badly want but cannot really afford. What do you do?
A. Go ahead and buy it regardless.
B. Forget about it for the time being.
C. Dither about buying it but say to yourself, 'I can always return it'.

2. Tragically, a child chokes on a piece of a toy and dies. What is your first reaction to this news item?
A. 'Toys are so shoddy these days; I bet it was from China.'
B. 'What could the parents have been thinking?'
C. 'What a terrible tragedy for the parents.'

3. There is something you think you require but don't need for at least a few days. What do you do?
A. Go out more or less immediately to get it.
B. Phone the shop and have it put to one side.
C. Visit the shop in a few days' time, when convenient.

4. You see a news item that puts someone in a bad light. It could be a rock star alleged to be drunk on a transatlantic flight. How do you respond?
A. Say to yourself, 'There's no smoke without fire'.
B. Wait until more facts come out.
C. Believe the worst.

5. You have a run-in with someone in a meeting. Afterwards, you are cross. What do you do?
A. Ring the person up straight away and have it out on the phone.
B. Put down in writing why you are cross.
C. Wait until the next time you meet that person and have it out then.

6. A public figure you dislike apparently does something that puts that person in a good light. How do you respond?
A. Say to yourself, 'Let's see what happens'.
B. Say to yourself that it's a flash in the pan.
C. Admit to yourself that you are pleasantly surprised.

Test 2

1. You are on holiday. It is raining when it is supposed to be sunny. How do you respond?
A. Moan until the cows come home to whoever will listen.
B. Write cards home saying that it is lovely weather for the ducks.
C. Find things to do where the rain does not spoil your pleasure.

2. Someone persists in calling you by a name you would rather not be called by, like a nickname you once had and thought you had lost. How do you respond?
A. Treat the whole thing as childish.
B. Make remarks the other person can hear without addressing her directly.
C. Call that person to her face by a name you know she would rather not be called.

3. You are driving on a dual carriageway where trucks – as they do – keep coming out and slowing down vehicles in the outside lane. How do you respond?

A. Accept the situation and sit tight.

B. When you come alongside the offending trucks, give them a blast on the horn.

C. Gesticulate to all and sundry that you are not happy.

4. Someone whose work you like says he or she can't do a job for you for three months – because of having too much on, etc. How do you respond?

A. Pester the person to do the work sooner.

B. Wait the three months.

C. Find someone else to do the work.

5. You are kept waiting in an airport shuttle bus for another passenger who is late. How do you respond?

A. Ask the driver repeatedly how long he or she will wait before leaving.

B. Sit back and read your book.

C. Make pointed remarks to the other passengers when the latecomer arrives.

6. You are in a queue. Another, parallel queue seems to be moving faster. How do you respond?

A. Stay in your queue and wait your turn.

B. Stay in your queue but look pointedly and repeatedly at your watch.

C. Switch to the other queue, disturbing others in the process.

Test 3

1. Someone you work alongside is under-performing and needs to be told. What do you do?

A. Leave it to someone else, like your boss, to have a word.

B. Tell the person in no uncertain terms to improve and say that you are not there to carry him or her.

C. Speak to the person, pointing out what the problem is and how it needs to be addressed.

2. You are in a department store trying to pay for your purchases. There is a long queue and only one person serving. How do you react?
A. Shout out to the person serving for more staff to be called.
B. When you reach the counter ask politely why more staff can't be put on when there is such a long queue.
C. When you reach the counter say pointedly that you have waited so long that you thought you would have to pay in euros.

3. You are served the wrong food in a restaurant. You are given something you never eat. How do you respond?
A. Push the offending food to one side and eat the rest telling the waiter when he asks that the food was fine.
B. Draw the waiter to one side and explain quietly what has happened.
C. Voice your displeasure so that everyone around hears.

4. You are in a cinema. Some people are whispering in the row behind you. It is bothering you. What do you do?
A. Turn your head slightly to one side and make a loud 'shush' noise.
B. Turn round and ask them if they would mind keeping quiet because they are spoiling the film for you.
C. Say nothing and hope they will stop.

5. You book into a hotel and find that the staff have overlooked your reservation although it turns out to be on the system. At first, the receptionist says that you can't be fitted in but later offers you a room in an annexe some way away. What do you do?
A. Say that you can't believe the way you are being treated and that you will certainly never use this hotel again.
B. Say that you booked the room and want what you booked – a room on this site – asking the receptionist to find one, please.
C. Take the room in the annexe.

6. You believe that a superior treated you unfairly in front of your colleagues. What do you do?
A. Make a point of snubbing the superior the next time you are together.
B. Let it go, believing that it won't happen again.
C. Explain to the superior the source of your grievance and say that you are looking for an apology.

Test 4

1. You want to go to bed but the group you are with is having a good time and wants to stay up. How do you respond?
A. Find a way of staying up until everyone is ready for bed.
B. Go to bed with earplugs or whatever, and try to sleep.
C. Go to bed, fail to sleep and get up to complain about the noise they are making.

2. You are interested in a cosmetic operation but are told that the outcome is uncertain and that the operation is not recommended to anyone who is risk-averse. How do you respond?
A. Go ahead with the operation and then complain when it goes wrong.
B. Wait until the success of the operation is more certain.
C. Ask yourself whether you really need the operation.

3. You are with a group who want to eat Chinese food. You really don't like Chinese food. What do you do?
A. Refuse point-blank to eat Chinese.
B. Try strenuously to persuade the rest of the group to eat elsewhere.
C. Eat Chinese with the group but get them to promise to let you choose where to eat the next time you go out together.

4. There is a house in a village you would like to buy but you have just realized that the heating fuel in the village is oil, not gas. You are not sure you like oil; it seems to be messy. How do you proceed?

A. Withdraw from the purchase of the property.
B. Try to haggle on the price using oil as the reason.
C. Review your reasons for wanting the house in the first place, asking yourself whether oil is really such a drawback and what compensations might outweigh it.

5. There is an event in southern Greece you would very much like to attend but you do not like flying. What do you do?
A. Abandon the idea.
B. Dismiss your fear of flying, bite the bullet, and fly.
C. Determine to drive, however time-consuming and inconvenient.

6. You are with a group that is following a pre-published programme. You, however, have things you would like to do while you are on this trip. How do you respond?
A. Criticize some of the activities in the presence of group members.
B. Keep to the programme and resolve to return without the company of an organized group.
C. Mix the programme and your activities even though doing that will bother the group leader and some of the group members.

Scoring your answers

For each of Tests 1–4 compare your answers with those given in the keys below. For each item put a ring round your answer. The totals will be the number of answers you have ringed in each column.

Test 1	Most EI	Least EI	Intermediate
Item 1	B	A	C
2	C	B	A
3	C	A	B
4	B	C	A
5	C	A	B
6	A	B	C
Totals			

Test 2	Most EI	Least EI	Intermediate
Item 1	C	A	B
2	A	B	C
3	A	B	C
4	B	C	A
5	B	C	A
6	A	C	B
Totals			

Test 3	Most EI	Least EI	Intermediate
Item 1	C	B	A
2	B	A	C
3	B	C	A
4	B	A	C
5	B	A	C
6	C	A	B
Totals			

Test 4	Most EI	Least EI	Intermediate
Item 1	A	C	B
2	C	A	B
3	C	A	B
4	C	A	B
5	B	A	C
6	B	C	A
Totals			

Self-awareness

By the end of this chapter, the aim is that you will have an understanding of what it is to be aware of your emotions and how adept you are at being self-aware. At a deeper level, you will recognize the power your inner feelings have to enrich your life experiences – something that must be acknowledged and appreciated if your EI is to be enhanced and developed.

The importance of self-knowledge

It is often said that increased self-knowledge and the pursuit of human happiness are inextricably linked – from one follows the other. Certainly it is hard to feel satisfied with your life if you are confused about who and what you are. This does not appear to have been the case with Screaming Lord Sutch – a minor 1960s rock star who contested one by-election after another once his musical career was over. As far as we can tell, it never bothered him when he came last in the poll, probably because he never expected to win. He seemed to know exactly what it was that he got out of dressing outrageously and repeatedly fighting lost causes. We imagine that he was motivated by the opportunities it gave to play the jester, thumb his nose at party politics, and to participate in the democratic process – or he may have just enjoyed being in the limelight.

But how many of us have that kind of understanding of our own feelings and impulses and are able to use that knowledge to help us make the important decisions that affect our lives, and to regulate and shape our behaviour? Experience suggests that we often have false and unrealistic perceptions about ourselves. At the two extremes, we are either too down on ourselves, or we are too full of self-regard. However, tough though it might be to admit it, working out exactly who you are is not purely a thinking matter. When you come to ponder plans or make decisions or embark on courses of action, who you are is defined as much as anything by the strength of your inner feelings. Hence, admirable though the impulse may be to want to succeed in other fields, you have to ask what is going on, not just in your head, but also in your emotions. What are we trying to prove to ourselves and to others? It is conventional wisdom to say that you should stick with what you do best – 'to stick with the knitting'. We need to take care therefore that, while recognizing their importance, we do not allow our emotions to skew our judgements.

Aspects of self-awareness

In Chapter 1 we broke down self-awareness into six key aspects as follows:

- Respect yourself.
- Be positive.
- Be true to yourself.
- Give logic and rationality a rest.
- Listen to others.
- Understand your impact on others.

We will now discuss these in more detail. You will find a test associated with each one at the end of the chapter.

Respect yourself

This aspect of self-awareness is about recognizing and respecting your own inner feelings, and in so doing taking care of yourself. Carl Rogers, a US psychologist, put it even more strongly. When writing about the lessons he had learnt from his own life, he said that he had come to accept his inner feelings and impulses 'as an enriching part of me'. He then went on to say that, 'I don't expect to act on all of them, but when I accept them all, I can be more real: my behaviour, therefore, will be more appropriate to the immediate situation'. In other words, accepting rather than denying our innermost feelings not only enhances our life experiences, but also improves the ways in which we behave.

Reflecting on your inner feelings

Take some time to reflect on the inner feelings and impulses, which have the capacity to be an 'enriching part' of you. Which do you accept and which do you deny? Which do you act on and which do you suppress?

So, our advice would be to exercise your right to look after 'number one' by attending to your own feelings and impulses even if that means spending less time fretting over the emotional needs of other people. All that sounds as if we are urging you to be self-centred – to be devoid of empathy (see Chapter 5) – but that is not what we mean. To be truly selfish would mean concentrating solely on your own emotional needs while ignoring the feelings of other people. What we are saying is that it is important to get the balance right between celebrating your own humanity by accepting your inner feelings, and respecting those of other people. From the point of view of EI, to worry continually about how other people are feeling is every bit as unhealthy as being obsessed with your own emotional self.

Thus, getting the balance right is the goal you should set yourself – a state that could result in your being 'comfortable with yourself'. But being at ease with emotions does not necessarily mean that you have achieved perfection – that the balance is right and that there is no room for improvement. What you could be really saying is, 'I know what and who I am and I accept it', which in turn could be interpreted as, 'I don't need to change'. If that is the case, the danger is that, in deceiving yourself, you are stagnating in terms of your emotional intelligence and in so doing missing an opportunity to grow and develop as an individual.

Be positive

Is the glass half empty or half full? You are being positive if you see it as being half full every time. An inclination towards negativity is emotionally disabling and ultimately it undermines the whole personality. To be fully self-aware is to be open to possibilities, and you can't be fully open to possibilities if for most of the time your mind is already closed. In terms of your EI it is healthy to be sceptical, but to be cynical is to be closed off – to be very cynical is even worse.

Suppose someone says that they know that they are 'a miserable so-and-so'. Do you credit that person with some self-awareness? Conceivably you might, but if you do, you should recognize that what that person is really doing is shutting down on much of what is possible. It is as if the person was actually saying, 'I know that I have my limitations, but I like it that way' – which, of course, is that person's prerogative. It cannot be denied that such people are self-aware – but only with respect to a diminished part of themselves. It is only by trying things out that you learn to define and then refine your tastes and preferences – and in so doing explore your own human potential. A refusal even to try leaves you a lesser person than you might be – someone who is not really sure of what you are capable of becoming. How many of us are prepared to push ourselves to the limit to find out what we can really do? However, in order to be positive you have to be self-aware – to have confidence in your own capabilities, but not to the point of mindless gung-ho optimism.

Downers

Think of negative people you know. The sort who start sentences with 'It's difficult' or 'There's no point'. What strikes you about them? Have they worked things out so that when they say 'No' you can be sure it is based on self-knowledge? Or is it that they turn things down in a blanket sort of way out of fear of the unknown? Suppose that they express their negative feelings in an amusing way (as they often do). Does that make them feel better about them-selves? Does it make you feel any better disposed towards them?

Make a note of any lessons that can be learnt from this exercise.

Finally, remember that being prejudiced – overtly or covertly – is another sure sign of negativity. This is because prejudice is about making judgements or forming opinions without due consideration of all the relevant information and the issues that it raises. The resultant bias and unthinking hostility rules out many constructive possibilities that would otherwise be open to you. This is because prejudices close our minds by crystallizing our negative feelings without subjecting them to a rigorous examination of their underlying causes and a close examination of their consequences for us and for other people.

Be true to yourself

This is about being authentic, doing things in keeping with whom and what you really are so that you can say to yourself, 'That's really me'. Of course, working this one out is not an easy thing to do because we are not accustomed to asking, 'Who am I?' One of us had a birthday recently and he wondered how to celebrate it – a big party or not. So, he talked to friends, who said, 'Big party, that's not you at all'. He then discussed it with the family and they said, 'Why not? You'll enjoy it.' So he had the party and thoroughly enjoyed it.

The real me?

Take a little time to ask yourself: What is the real me? What defines me? When am I being true to myself, and when am I not being true to myself? You will probably need to take your time with this exercise because the answers are unlikely to come quickly, but we believe you will find it to be both rewarding and illuminating.

Just because you enjoyed a party doesn't turn you overnight from being an introvert into an extrovert – there is much more to being true to yourself than that. What you have to work out is what does and does not suit you most of the time. By all means 'go with the flow', but when there comes a real sticking point – when you feel you are behaving in ways which are out of keeping with the real you – then the time has come to say 'enough is enough'.

Being true to yourself, therefore, is about being realistic – knowing the strength and limitations of your feelings and acting accordingly. In this respect, the first thing to grasp is that being true to yourself does not diminish you; rather, it sharpens your perception of the range of options open to you so that you get fewer disappointments and more success in your life. If you know you don't enjoy working with other people, try to find something else in which you have an opportunity to do more things on your own. If you know that voluntary work is not for you, steer clear of it and find some other outlet for your energies that will give you greater satisfaction. If you have always had a yen to do so, run a marathon by all means, but if you are a fun-runner, make sure that you have some fun.

Give logic and rationality a rest

This aspect of self-awareness is neatly encapsulated by the title of a song by David Byrne, 'Stop Making Sense'. Put simply, the advice here is to be more receptive to what your emotions are telling you – to take your 'gut feelings' seriously. To do this you have to be prepared to banish the brain tyrant and surrender yourself to your intuitions, sensations and the play of your imagination.

The song, therefore, serves to warn us against allowing rationality to frame our lives even when our emotions try to drive it out. However inept we may be at it, great store is placed in our society on the powers of rational thought. As a result, the creative, playful side of most of us is under-utilized and under-nourished. Most people have learnt to suppress their intuition, and are conditioned to rely solely on the logical, rational parts of their mind. Intuition, by the way, means the power or faculty of attaining to direct knowledge or cognition without evident rational thought and inference – in other words, having a thought without knowing how that thought came into your head. The role of intuition in empathy as a component of EI is discussed in Chapter 5.

Thus, when people say 'get in touch with yourself', what they are telling us is to connect with intuitive and creative parts of our minds. Of course, getting in touch with yourself has a lot to do with discovering who you are, and being true to yourself. Just how you get in touch with yourself is a very individual thing. For example, a doctor friend of one of us – as rational and efficient as you like – discovered that the only way of responding to the emotions provoked by the tragedy in New York on 11 September 2001 was to take up painting. Very quickly she produced a series of canvasses, but she could barely explain where they had come from; logic was no help there.

Listen to others

The line of argument here is that by closing your ears to others, you are, in effect, seriously restricting the possibility of reflecting on your own feelings, thoughts and behaviour. The more self-absorbed you are, the less self-aware you are likely to be – you lose that balance we talked about earlier. People who do not listen think that they know best – 'Minds like beds always made up', in William Carlos Williams' phrase. People who think that they know best are refusing to reflect on their own behaviour except perhaps to confirm that they still know best.

But to improve in the self-awareness component of EI demands more than just listening; you have to avoid passing judgement or drawing conclusions prematurely, or responding defensively to what is being said. The more you fail to avoid these reactions, the more frustrated, agitated and angry (and the less self-controlled) you are likely to become. Perhaps that is why some people cease to listen. But it is not the answer – you have to listen actively and openly and try to make sense of what you have heard. The importance of communicating effectively with others as an aspect of the social skills component of EI is discussed in more detail in Chapter 6.

Understand your impact on others

Understanding your impact on others is a crucial aspect of self-awareness because strong feelings and the impulses they generate can be explosive if handled incorrectly. We have to be wary of the way we respond to our own emotions, therefore, as well as being sensitive to those of other people. But how many of us really understand the impact we have on others, including those who are closest to us? We might come across to some as being distant and insensitive, to others as devious and shifty, and as all of these things to some people. We might be shocked if we ever found out what others really think and feel about us – and it is a curiosity of human behaviour that we rarely do find out. For example, can you honestly say, hand on heart, that you understand what colleagues and acquaintances feel about you – even the ones you think of as being close to you? Is the inner you truly an unknown land?

Often we only find out something about ourselves when a person blurts something out inadvertently. It may not be pleasant finding information out this way (depending on what they have to say). You can learn things about yourself by asking directly, but that may not come easily to you. It is worth trying, however, with someone who knows you well and whose judgements you respect. With the advent in the workplace of 360-degree evaluation and appraisal, more and more people are being asked to pass judgement on others (and on themselves) by means of specially designed inventories and questionnaires. Since such evaluations are meant to be both anonymous and confidential, you should be able to place a degree of trust in what other people are saying about you. However, the exercise will only be of value to you if you are willing to reflect on (and, where appropriate, act on) the feedback it provides.

So, it can be tricky to find out exactly how we impact on other people, and so we have to learn to monitor our own behaviour as best we can. That is where empathy – our ability to sense how other people are feeling – helps (see Chapter 5). If you can sense with a degree of accuracy how others are feeling, then you can usually gauge how they are responding to you, and in that way make sure that you behave in ways that are appropriate for the circumstances.

The tests

For every **item** in each of the six **tests** choose **one** answer by circling A, B or C. Remember, in the cause of accuracy of assessment we are asking you to circle the action closest to what you would do, or have been doing. Do not opt for what you now think is the best or most admirable thing to do. After all, to want to put yourself in the most favourable light is hardly an emotionally intelligent way of responding. A key is provided at the end of the tests which will enable you to score your answers.

Test 1

1. Some friends ask you to look after their cat while they go on holiday for a week. You are not fond of pets. How do you respond?
A. Say that you'd love to, but remind them what you are like with animals.
B. After a few moans and groans say that you'll do it.
C. Say that you've made a rule not to look after pets, and that you apply that rule equally to all your friends.

2. A friend you believed to be close suddenly breaks off all communication for no apparent reason. You are puzzled and phone and write but get no reply. What do you do?
A. Reason that a true friend will get back in touch and wait for that to happen.
B. Continue writing and phoning, asking what's wrong and saying how upset you are at the lack of response.
C. Contact some mutual friends to try to get to the bottom of it.

3. A friend says you are looking under the weather and suggests you go to the doctor. How do you respond?
A. Say OK, maybe it's for the best and that you have been feeling off-colour.
B. Say you'll go but that you're not expecting anything.
C. Ask what the point is when all they do is say the same old thing and send you off with some pills to swallow.

4. You suffer a number of setbacks at something you have been good at. How do you respond?
A. Say to yourself that you must have 'lost it'.
B. Say to yourself that you haven't suddenly become poor at this overnight and that the knack will return.
C. Say to yourself that if only others would help you more, you could get back to where you were.

5. You meet a couple at a party you haven't seen for at least five years. The first thing they do is to make a personal remark about your appearance. How do you respond?
A. Respond tit for tat with a personal remark.
B. Decide that they have blurted it out on account of being flustered, and let the remark pass.
C. Counter by saying to them that they always did make personal remarks and that nothing has changed.

6. Something you badly wanted fails to materialize. How do you respond?
A. Say to yourself that there'll be other opportunities in the future.
B. Say to yourself that it wasn't meant to happen on this occasion.
C. Say to yourself that you shouldn't have set your heart on the thing in the first place.

Test 2

1. A job comes up. For you to do it would be a bit of a stretch but someone you trust suggests that you put your name forward. How do you respond?
A. Decide that you are not sure, and that you will have a better chance next time.
B. Decide that it's too much of a stretch and don't apply.
C. Say to yourself, 'Why not? What's the worst that could happen?' and put your name forward.

2. You fail in something that is quite new to you. How do you respond?
A. Conclude that the odds were stacked against you.
B. Tell yourself that you've learnt from the experience and that you'll know how to succeed next time.
C. Tell yourself that you gave it your best shot.

3. A company offers you a free sample of a new product plus a larger amount of the product, which you can buy or return. How do you respond?
A. Say there must be a catch and decline the offer.
B. Accept the offer and try the product.
C. Accept the offer then change your mind and send the product back untouched.

4. Someone fails to turn up at a meeting with you for the second time. How do you do respond?
A. Find a way of getting your own back – rearrange the meeting but don't turn up.
B. Give that person one more chance – rearrange the meeting.
C. Drop that person from your life – don't rearrange the meeting.

5. A certain professional tennis player is always talking about taking positives from his matches, even when he receives a thrashing. When you hear that kind of talk, how do you respond?
A. Reason that he has to take what positives he can from his matches as long as he intends to play top tennis.
B. Decide that he is talking garbage – he's a loser.
C. Conclude that he's just trying to keep his spirits up after a heavy defeat.

6. When you are thrown together with new people how do you typically respond?
A. You're shy and say as little as possible.
B. You're wary and guarded and wait for people to approach you.
C. You're open and friendly unless something happens to change that.

Test 3

1. The invitation to a gathering says 'smart casual'. You are inclined to be smart but friends who are also going indicate that they will be dressing quite casually. What do you decide to do?
A. Find an excuse not to go.
B. Dress quite casually so that you don't look any different from your friends.
C. Trust your own judgement – dress smartly.

2. You start doing something because you like the idea of it, like learning a musical instrument. You find yourself struggling. How do you respond?
A. Abandon what you are doing in favour of something you are likely to be good at.
B. Keep going regardless.
C. Find a new teacher.

3. A friend asks you what you want out of life. How do you respond?
A. Say, 'I pretty much always know what I want'.
B. Say, 'I'm never sure what I want'.
C. Say, 'Sometimes I know what I want, other times I'm not sure'.

4. Think of some activities you find yourself doing even though you don't want to do them – maybe related to your job, a particular aspect of your job, or something in your spare time. When it is pointed out to you that you are doing these things although you don't want to, how do you respond?
A. Say that you mean to do things differently from now on.
B. Say that you intend to soldier on.
C. Say that you are going to take stock of your position.

5. Some friends keep telling you that you are a good cook and urge you to take it up professionally. This has never crossed your mind. You just think of yourself as a good cook, and have no illusions about your talent. How do you respond to what these friends have said to you?
A. Stick to the 'day job' and continue giving pleasure to friends.
B. Spend time trying to work out what would be involved in quitting your job and becoming a cook.
C. Spend time getting together a collection of your recipes then send it to professional cooks and publishers.

6. Think of a past achievement that, in the cold light of day, you might have to accept is now beyond you. When the subject of whether you could still do this comes up, how do you respond?
A. Say to yourself, 'Why not? Why not me? Anyone can dream.'
B. Say to yourself that you are not ruling anything out.
C. Say to yourself that it is now definitely beyond you.

Test 4

1. Suppose you are given the choice of conventional or alternative medicine or both. How do you respond?
A. Pick and mix according to what you think might be wrong with you.
B. Look seriously at alternative – maybe conventional has reached its limits.
C. Go for the conventional every time – alternative is for cranks.

2. Chatting with new acquaintances, you are asked what you do in your spare time – how you (literally!) take your mind off things. How do you respond?
A. Say that you have one, maybe two different ways to relax.
B. Say that you have several different ways to relax.
C. Say that you find it hard to relax.

3. There was a film with Arnold Schwarzenegger as a pregnant man. How do you respond to that?
A. Great off-the-wall idea having a male actor pregnant, especially Arnie.
B. It's just another gimmicky vehicle for Arnie.
C. Don't buy the premise; it's just not believable.

4. A newspaper columnist asserts that everyday superstitions like not walking under a ladder and throwing a pinch of salt over your left shoulder are childlike and ridiculous. Would you:
A. Do both of those mentioned, and one or two others?
B. Do lots of things like that, because you don't regard them as superstitions?
C. Do none of those, nor would you ever?

5. Being creative means making things: words, music, objects. A survey question asks how much of your spare time you spend being creative. How do you respond?
A. Say that making things dominates your waking time.
B. Say that you spend a little time, here and there, being creative.
C. Say that you never do anything creative.

6. A talking point is whether it is absurd for scientists to believe in God. Where do you stand?
A. Disagree on the grounds that until the origins of life are established beyond doubt (which will never happen), the existence of God cannot be ruled out.
B. Agree with the view that science is rational and that anything else is superstition.
C. State that you are undecided and that you like to think you are rational but have a spiritual side.

Test 5

1. Someone offers an opinion that is quite contrary to something you feel strongly about. How do you respond?

A. Hear the other person out and then respond.
B. Listen for a while, and then reject it.
C. Reject the opposing view outright.

2. You are with a long-winded person who is taking an awfully long time to cough up whatever it is they want to say. How do you respond?
A. Lose interest after a while and walk away.
B. Raise a hand to get their attention and when they pause ask politely what point they are making.
C. Interrupt them with an 'Excuse me' once you conclude they are struggling.

3. When you are not sure what to do, how do you proceed?
A. Work it out for yourself, however long it takes.
B. Ask around for advice.
C. Look up a book or the Web.

4. Think of the last five conversations you had and try to remember what was said to you – not the exact words but the gist. How much do you remember?
A. Very little if anything.
B. Some of it.
C. All or nearly all of it.

5. A survey question asks how you feel about listening to others. How do you respond?
A. Say that people are very predictable – you can always tell what they are going to say.
B. Say that, by and large, you're not interested in what other people have to say.
C. Suggest that it's how people say things as much as what they say that counts.

6. When you are communicating with other people, what goes through your mind?
A. Nothing goes through your mind particularly.

B. That other people are different from you in certain distinct ways – softer, tougher, fussier, funnier, stupider etc.
C. That they are no different from you.

Test 6

1. A colleague challenges you to name your worst fault. How do you respond?
A. Say that you're not sure what it is.
B. Say that you know what it is, that it's pretty bad, but you're working on it.
C. Say that your worst fault is hardly a fault at all.

2. To your surprise, someone gives you a label you have never been given before – it might be 'nice' or 'sweet' or 'tough' or 'shy'. How do you react?
A. Ask them why they are calling you that.
B. Accept the label for the time being but make it clear that you are sceptical.
C. Protest that they don't know you and ask how they can say that.

3. You participate significantly in some kind of event – it might be at work, a sporting occasion or a live performance. After it is over, what do you do?
A. Tell anyone who will listen what it was like for you.
B. Don't speak to anyone about it.
C. Ask people whose opinions you value what they thought.

4. A survey question asks why you think people stay friends with you. How do you respond?
A. Say that they like you because you like them.
B. Say that they like you because of what you are – warts and all.
C. Say that they like you because they've always been your friends.

5. Chatting with friends, one of them asks you to name your best characteristic. How do you respond?
A. Say that you're not sure what it is.
B. Say that you know what it is and that you're still working on it.
C. Say that you don't have a best – or worst – characteristic.

6. Think of a couple of people who you suspect do not like you. How are you going to deal with them?
A. Try to get them to like you.
B. Ask them to their face if they don't like you and, if so, why.
C. Leave things as they are.

Scoring your answers

For each of Tests 1–6 compare your answers with those given in the keys below. For each item put a ring round your answer. The totals will be the number of answers you have ringed in each column.

Test 1	Most EI	Least EI	Intermediate
Item 1	C	B	A
2	A	B	C
3	A	C	B
4	B	A	C
5	B	A	C
6	A	C	B
Totals			

Test 2	Most EI	Least EI	Intermediate
Item 1	C	B	A
2	B	A	C
3	B	A	C
4	B	A	C
5	A	B	C
6	C	A	B
Totals			

Test 3	Most EI	Least EI	Intermediate
Item 1	C	A	B
2	A	B	C
3	A	B	C
4	A	B	C
5	A	C	B
6	C	A	B
Totals			

Test 4	Most EI	Least EI	Intermediate
Item 1	B	C	A
2	B	C	A
3	A	B	C
4	B	C	A
5	A	C	B
6	A	B	C
Totals			

Test 5	Most EI	Least EI	Intermediate
Item 1	A	C	B
2	B	A	C
3	B	A	C
4	C	A	B
5	C	B	A
6	B	A	C
Totals			

Test 6	Most EI	Least EI	Intermediate
Item 1	B	C	A
2	A	C	B
3	C	A	B
4	B	C	A
5	B	C	A
6	B	A	C
Totals			

Motivation

Put simply, motivation refers to the forces that energize and direct behaviour, that help us, individually and in groups, to achieve our goals. What we are talking about here is self-confidence, drive, determination, persistence, commitment and optimism.

Like all the elements of EI, motivation should never be thought of as operating in isolation. Evidently we need to be sufficiently self-aware in order to appreciate what it is that drives us to achieve (or under-achieve) from time to time and in different situations. Similarly, we have to be able to control and regulate our own emotional energies in order to perform to the best of our ability, especially when under pressure.

We also need to be sensitive to what it is that motivates others if we are to influence their behaviour as individuals and as groups. In addition, an understanding of motivation has an important contribution to make to the development of our social skills including our ability to have a positive effect on the behaviour of others, avoid and resolve conflicts, live and work collaboratively with people, exercise leadership and contribute to building and sustaining successful teams.

Incentives and motives

An incentive is a reward offered to an individual or group in order to induce the person(s) to work harder, perform better or learn more effectively – in short, to persuade him, her or them to behave in a preferred way. Its objective, therefore, is to motivate. Praise, rewards, prizes, honours and bonuses are commonly used as incentives in a wide variety of circumstances ranging from the relationships between two people (eg parent and child) through to how a large corporation seeks to manage the performance of its workforce. In the short term, deterrents such as scolding, penalties and punishments may have the same effect, but the chances are that they will eventually induce behaviours that are the opposite of those intended – that is, they will demotivate rather than motivate. Using deterrents and incentives in conjunction with each other, as is usually done, is often referred to as adopting a 'carrot and stick' approach to motivation.

Carrots and sticks

Think about how incentives are used to motivate individuals or groups in a situation with which you are familiar (eg a family, a team, a school or a workplace).

- What incentives are used?
- Who uses them?
- How are they used?
- What are they hoping to achieve by using them?
- How do they influence behaviour?
- Is there a difference between their short-term and their long-term effects?

Repeat the exercise, but this time think about the use of criticism, scolding and punishments. Finally, draw up a list of the ways in which the two methods (incentives and deterrents) seem to influence your own responses to them, including in situations in which the two are used together.

'Extrinsic' and 'intrinsic' motivation

A common feature of incentives and deterrents is that they are being used in an attempt to drive behaviour from outside, and not from within individuals or groups. It is important, therefore, to distinguish between motivation that is a response to incentives and inducements offered by others, and that which comes from within us. The former is normally referred to as 'extrinsic motivation' whereas that which is generated internally is known as 'intrinsic motivation'. In order to behave in an emotionally intelligent way you need to be able to recognize how, in any given situation, your behaviour, and that of others, may be being driven – sometimes in different directions – by the complex interplay of motives originating from these two sources. So let us explore them a little further.

If you reflect on what it is that drives you and members of your family, friends, co-workers, team-mates to behave in certain ways, you will probably conclude that much depends upon the circumstances. For example, let's take those individuals who find it difficult to motivate themselves while at school or in the workplace – perhaps you are among them. Those responsible for your performance (eg teachers, supervisors and managers) will probably deploy a whole range of strategies and tactics in an attempt to increase your motivation to learn or to work more effectively. These are likely to include a mixture of 'carrots' and 'sticks', including such inducements as reminders about future benefits that will accrue from increased effort, such as better examination results, a place at university, salary increases and improved job prospects. The promise of 'jam tomorrow' is likely to be accompanied by dire warnings about the consequences of a continued lack of effort and commitment: 'Mark my words, you'll live to regret it.'

All of this falls within the 'extrinsic' category of motivation because both the inducements and the deterrents come from sources outside the individual. They are likely to be more or less effective depending on how skilfully and sensitively they are used, and by whom. This is because, for whatever reason, we are all capable of responding differently to the same message coming from different people. That is why some teachers are able to motivate students who are reluctant to learn where others fail to do so, and why some managers of teams resign or are sacked because they can no longer motivate their players – 'I've taken them as far as I can', they are often reported as saying.

Learning from someone else's experience

Talk to someone you know who is more experienced than yourself and who is acknowledged as being successful in their chosen career. Try to find out from this person what it is that has motivated him or her to achieve. For example, where in this individual's personal list does he or she place the following drivers:

- status and material gains;
- the challenge of doing a job well;
- fear of failure;
- working with people;
- responding to change;
- interest and stimulation?

Are there any lessons that you can draw from this person's experience?

Paradoxically, those same individuals who demonstrate a lack of motivation at school or at work are often capable of concentrating for hours on end in their own time when engaged in tasks or activities that happen to interest them. For these people – and many of us share this characteristic – their drive and commitment appear to come from within themselves, fuelled by the personal pleasure and inner satisfaction they derive from what they are doing.

There are of course individuals – you may be one of them – who derive the same sort of inner rewards from their work. Job satisfaction seems to be the basis of the 'sense of vocation' that drives some people to seek out a career in a particular occupation such as nursing or teaching, despite the fact that the status and material rewards may well be greater in other professions. This is not to say that traditional incentives are not important to these people, but that the source of their most powerful motivation is internal and not external.

'Great work starts with great feelings' (Daniel Goleman)

Keep a log over the course of a week in which you make a careful note of how you feel when you are engaged in different tasks at work, when studying, and during your leisure activities. Then consider the following:

- In which of your activities did you feel most interested and disinterested?
- From which activities did you derive the greatest and least pleasure?
- Did any of the activities prove to be stressful or irritating? Did any of them make you feel happy, upbeat?
- Can you see any patterns in the way you feel about the different activities in which you were engaged?

Does your analysis tell you anything about your own motivation? Now think about the implications for you of what Goleman said in the quotation given above.

Aspects of motivation

The emphasis here is on your motivation and on how it influences your personal behaviour; we will deal in later chapters with motivation as a component in empathy and social skills. You will recall that in Chapter 1 we broke motivation down into four key aspects:

- striving to improve and to achieve high standards;
- being committed to achieving your goals;
- taking the initiative and seizing opportunities;
- being optimistic even in the face of adversity.

We will now discuss these in more detail. You will find a test associated with each one at the end of the chapter.

Striving to improve and to achieve high standards

Individuals who are strong in this aspect of motivation are characterized by being goal oriented: unlike lesser mortals, they always seem to know exactly what it is that they are seeking to achieve. Having a clear sense of their aims and objectives is coupled with a determination to set themselves high standards – there are no easy targets or 'soft options' for them. What this means is that they are not content to reach a comfortable plateau with regard to what they have achieved; they are always eager to set themselves the challenge of scaling new heights.

Any given Sunday

This is an exercise probably for a Sunday. On any given Sunday (which happens to be the name of a film about American football) watch the end of a big sporting event on TV such as a tennis tournament or golf championship. When interviewed, what do the winners and the losers have to say? What does it tell you about their motivation to succeed and to perform well? Is there anything that you can learn from them?

High-performing individuals are also prepared to take calculated risks when others might err towards caution. This is not to
say that they are prepared to gamble everything on lost causes,
but they are willing to assess the evidence, then back their own
judgement and their ability to succeed. They also treat information as an asset – the basis of good decision-making. This
means that they are willing to seek out extra data and other
points of view when others would be content with what they
have already. Finally, whatever standards of excellence they
have reached, they still aspire to improve. To that end, they seek
feedback on their performance if that is not forthcoming. Look
at how top golfers or tennis players change their coaches if they
feel that a new voice with new ideas can help them perform at
even higher levels.

Being committed to achieving your goals

Commitment is widely recognized as a crucial component of
motivation – those who lack it (however talented they may
be) rarely achieve their full potential. On the other hand, time
and time again both individuals and groups with much less
innate ability demonstrate, through their commitment and
determination to succeed, that they are capable of achieving
at a much higher standard. Just think about all those bright
'stars' at junior school who end up being out-performed later
in life by individuals who at one time seemed to be much less
able. A visit to a school reunion can be full of surprises of
that nature. Just how well did the students regarded as being
the ones 'most likely to succeed' achieve once they left
school?

So, why do all those predictions seem to go wrong? Well, for
one thing people do grow and develop differently – the 'late
developer' being as well known a phenomenon as the 'child
prodigy'. However, the key is often commitment, ie the willingness of individuals and groups to make what other people
might see as 'sacrifices' in order to achieve their goals. Those
sacrifices can take many different forms, such as the long hours

of practice needed to become a successful musician, and the years of dedicated study that it takes to become a surgeon.

For some, it can also mean devoting time and emotional energy to personal relationships and caring for others as opposed to a career full of glittering prizes. Whatever the source of their motivation, those with commitment are the ones who are willing to devote the time and the effort needed to achieve their chosen objectives. Individuals such as these feel strongly – even passionately – about what it is they are seeking to achieve. Their commitment, therefore, is emotional.

The same can be said of those people who day in and day out demonstrate their commitment to the groups, teams and organizations of which they are members. They have strong attachments to the people with whom they are affiliated, and a firm commitment to shared values and goals, which are greater than any financial incentives. It is not surprising, therefore, to find that they are the ones who are willing to 'go the extra mile' for the common good, such as working unsocial hours in order to meet an important deadline. For many, their commitment is ideological: they believe in what they and their colleagues are doing, whether it be making a product of which they are proud or providing a service that they regard as being of value to their clients. Their beliefs, therefore, help to fuel their commitment. However, high levels of commitment and a desire to achieve high standards come at a price for the individuals concerned. The cost is often in terms of the impact that the demands of a career make on their personal lives and relationships or vice versa.

Because of the tension and inner turmoil that it can cause, the so-called 'life–work balance' is well worth examining. Some suggestions as to how you might do this are given below. Our experience suggests that unless you have thought through fundamental questions of this kind it will be difficult for you to have the conviction, clarity of purpose and inner belief that you need in order to succeed.

What do I want to achieve in life?

Consider the following list of life goals. Pick out the ones that are important to you. Now put them in rank order starting with the one that you regard as being the most important.

- to become a famous celebrity;
- to fulfil my potential;
- to earn as high a salary as possible;
- to indulge myself and to have as much pleasure as possible;
- to enjoy friendship and good companionship;
- to be independent and free from the demands of other people;
- to help the disadvantaged;
- to reach a position of power and authority;
- to make my parents proud of my achievements;
- to be a good parent and partner;
- to have a satisfying and worthwhile career;
- to have a secure and trouble-free life;
- other goals (add your own).

When you have made your list you should ask yourself a number of questions such as: Are you devoting your time and energy to achieving those things that you think are really important to you? If so, what are the consequences? What aspirations have you not yet fulfilled? Are you prepared to pay the price in order to achieve them?

Taking the initiative and seizing opportunities

Typically, those with strengths in this aspect of motivation are ready to take advantage of opportunities that help them to achieve their goals. They are generally more adept than other people at recognizing those opportunities in the first place, as well as appreciating their significance. Indeed, their optimism is such that they have a tendency to see a threat or setback as a challenge and hence as a chance to progress.

To make the point, consider how different airlines responded to the events in New York and Washington on 11 September 2001. Some of the companies made immediate plans to cut back their services and to make economies; others – the so-called 'no frills' airlines – reduced their fares and announced expansion plans. Six months later the former had in fact contracted, whereas the latter were developing additional services and placing orders for new planes.

Those individuals whose personal attributes include this kind of initiative are also prepared to persist when others are ready to give up. The old adage 'if at first you don't succeed try, try again' can be applied to them, and it is this kind of determination that underpins the ability to find new ways of solving technical problems or meeting clients' needs. Thus, when faced with established working practices and rules and regulations that are preventing them from getting on with the job in hand, these go-getters are skilled at devising and implementing creative ways of getting round them. For them it would seem that necessity is the mother of invention. Because their initiative, persistence and enterprise is often coupled with an enthusiasm for what they are doing, such people are usually good at winning the support and cooperation of others.

Being optimistic even in the face of adversity

If you are strong in this aspect of motivation, you possess personal attributes that enable you to continue to seek to achieve your goals even though you face difficulties and setbacks. The response of Steve Waugh on being dropped as the captain of Australia for one-day cricket matches illustrates these qualities. On hearing the news, he is reported to have said, 'This I see as a setback and a challenge. I don't believe I've lost value to the one-day side. I still believe I'm good enough to play for Australia. It's now my job to go out there and prove that.'

In making that statement he was reiterating his belief in his own ability, stating that he saw the setback as a challenge and indicating that it was up to him to prove to others that he was still good enough to play for his country. Everything he said was positive and optimistic – this was not the time for negative thoughts. With regard to his future actions it was clear that the anticipation of success in achieving his goal was at the forefront of his mind rather than the fear of failure.

At times of setbacks, therefore, optimists adopt the advice given in the words of an old song: 'accentuate the positive, eliminate the negative'. Consequently, they have a tendency to see failure to achieve their goals as being a consequence of circumstances beyond their control rather than as personal weakness.

The tests

For every **item** in each of the **tests** choose **one** answer by circling option A, B or C. Remember, in the cause of accuracy of assessment, you should circle the action closest to what you would do, or have been doing. Do not opt for what you now think is the best or most admirable thing to do. After all, to want to put yourself in the most favourable light is hardly an emotionally intelligent way of responding. A key is provided at the end of the tests which will enable you to score your answers.

Test 1

1. You feel frustrated and irritated by a difficult task that you have been asked to do. How do you respond?
A. Take a short break from it to clear your mind and to devise a plan for tackling the job effectively.
B. Keep your frustration to yourself, and get on with it as best you can.
C. Grumble about it to anyone who will listen and get it over with as quickly as you can.

2. You are working on an important task which you used to find interesting but you have done it so often that you are now bored with it. How do you respond?
A. Think out a way of doing it as quickly and effectively as possible on this occasion, and then explore the possibility of a 'job swap'.
B. Put it to the bottom of the pile and get on with other, more interesting things.
C. Get on with it, but give minimal time and attention to it.

3. You have worked hard to achieve your targets and find that you have exceeded them. How do you respond?
A. Enjoy the moment and then sit back and rest on your laurels.
B. Build on your success by setting yourself some new goals to aim for.
C. Maintain your effort so that your performance does not slip back from the standard you have established.

4. You have come up with some ideas for solving a problem but have been told by others that your ideas have little chance of success. How do you respond?
A. Think about what the others have said, modify your ideas, and then take a calculated risk of putting them into practice.
B. Bow to the others' superior judgement and forget all about it.
C. Ignore their advice, trust your own judgement and get on with it.

5. You have been working on something for a period of time and are having difficulty in judging how well you are doing and how you might improve. How do you respond?
A. Just carry on with what you were doing because no one to date has criticized your performance.
B. Trust your own judgement and modify your actions accordingly.
C. Carry out a self-evaluation, discuss it with someone whose judgement you trust, and modify your actions accordingly.

6. You are checking through some data with a view to making a decision and realize that some important bits of information are missing. How do you respond?
A. Assume that the missing data is unimportant and make a decision on the basis of the information at your disposal.
B. Take the trouble to chase up the missing data and only make a decision when all of it is available to you.
C. Make an informed guess about the missing information and make your decision accordingly.

Test 2

1. You have been asked to work on a task you dislike intensely. How do you respond?
A. Do it as quickly as you can but with minimum effort.
B. Keep putting it off in favour of tasks on which you prefer to work.
C. Get on with it to the best of your ability, giving it as much time and effort as you are able.

2. You are working on an important task and your colleagues ask you to break off to go for an early-evening drink. How do you respond?
A. Thank them for asking and explain why you can't go with them on this occasion.
B. Turn down their invitation flat without thanks.
C. Say that you will join them later if you can, even though you have no intention of doing so.

3. You are faced with a long and difficult task that requires hard work and painstaking attention to detail to achieve your goal. Someone suggests a quick and easy way of doing it. How do you respond?
A. Give careful consideration to the advice, but reject anything that might jeopardize the standard of your work.
B. Ignore the advice and stick to the tried and true method of doing the job irrespective of how long it takes.
C. Take up the suggestion immediately and get the job done as quickly as you can.

4. You have been asked to take on an extra responsibility that you know is important to your team, but you think that you will find the new role difficult. How do you respond?
A. Agree to take it on, but with no intention of giving it priority over your existing commitments.
B. Turn down the request on the grounds that you have more than enough to do already.
C. Say that despite the hard work that the extra responsibility entails, you are ready to face up to the new challenge.

5. The team of which you are a member has been successful even though your part in its achievements has been minor. How do you respond?
A. Show your pleasure at the team's achievements and pride in your own contribution, however minor.
B. Congratulate your team-mates and then get on with what you were doing, leaving them to celebrate their achievement.
C. Refuse to join in the celebrations on the grounds that you had little to do with the team's success.

6. You have been working very hard over a period of months in an attempt to improve your performance, but with little evidence to date that you are succeeding. How do you respond?
A. Keep going in the belief that you are right to set yourself high goals and that you will reach them in due course.
B. Reduce your efforts on the grounds that you can perform at a level that satisfies other people without having to try so hard.
C. Reaffirm your commitment to achieving your goals, but seek to improve the methods you are using to achieve them.

Test 3

1. A problem has come to light in something on which your team is working and you think you can help them to resolve it. How do you respond?

A. Put forward your ideas before anyone else has a chance to get in ahead of you.
B. Wait to be asked if you have any ideas for solving the problem.
C. Set out your ideas to the team with confidence and ask them to help you to implement them.

2. You are a member of a group in which no one will volunteer to take on an important task. You are confident that you could do it well. How do you respond?
A. Do nothing – wait to be asked.
B. Let it be known to the group that you would be willing to take on the task, and that with their support you are confident in your ability to do it well.
C. Don't hesitate – volunteer to do the job without consulting anyone.

3. A vacancy has occurred for a job that would require you to take on extra work and responsibility. How do you respond?
A. Don't apply – you can do without the hassle.
B. Show that you have confidence in your own ability by submitting your application for the job.
C. Wait to see if someone more experienced or better qualified than you are decides to apply.

4. A high-profile working party is being set up to investigate ways of tackling a problem. You have not been asked to join, but understand that volunteers may be considered. How do you respond?
A. Don't volunteer on the grounds that if you haven't been asked to join already, someone must think that you are not really cut out for it.
B. Put your name forward to serve on the group and let it be known that you are confident in your ability to make a positive contribution to its work.
C. Let it be known that if no one else volunteers you will be willing to do so.

5. You can see that a crisis is developing and no one present seems willing to take control of the situation. How do you respond?
A. Take the initiative yourself by assuming control of the situation until the necessary support arrives.
B. As quickly as you can find someone who is capable of taking control of the situation.
C. Mind your own business – you don't want to get the blame if something goes seriously wrong.

6. You have been asked if you would be willing to attend an event as back-up to the main team even though the chances are that you will not be called upon to do anything. How do you respond?
A. Accept the invitation as a chance to be involved and to learn from what will be a new experience.
B. Turn down the invitation on the grounds that your time would be better spent doing something more productive.
C. Accept the invitation but let it be known that you would rather be doing something else.

Test 4

1. Some unexpected bad news has left you and your colleagues feeling anxious and depressed about future prospects. How do you respond?
A. Suggest that you all go out for the evening and forget about it while you have a good time.
B. Allow yourself to be drawn into the general mood of pessimism.
C. Do your best to stay cheerful and concentrate your thoughts on trying to find ways of turning the situation to your advantage.

2. You have been given some negative feedback on your performance, which you were not expecting. How do you respond?

A. Listen to the criticisms without comment, but inwardly reject them.

B. Flatly refuse to accept the evidence on which the feedback is based.

C. Listen carefully to the feedback and consider ways in which you can use it alongside your own evaluation to improve your performance.

3. Despite your best efforts you are persistently failing to meet the performance targets you have set for yourself. How do you respond?

A. Stick to your performance targets, but re-examine the ways in which you are seeking to achieve them, if necessary increasing your efforts.

B. Refuse to give up and resolve to try harder in future.

C. Reschedule your performance targets downwards to a level that you know you can achieve.

4. Without warning, you have been asked to change the role in the team you are familiar with for one that will be new to you. How do you respond?

A. Turn it down on the grounds that it is unfair to expect you to take on new responsibilities at short notice.

B. Discuss what the new role would entail, then after due consideration back your own ability to respond to the challenge by accepting the job.

C. Agree to do the job for a trial period if certain conditions are met.

5. You are working to a strict deadline on an important project when you run into an unexpected problem. How do you respond?

A. Do what it takes to complete the project on time to the highest possible standard.

B. Explain the circumstances and make a plea for extra time to complete the work to your satisfaction.

C. Keep quiet about it and settle for doing the best that you can in the circumstances, cutting corners if necessary.

6. You have had a job interview, but were unsuccessful even though you appeared to be the best-qualified candidate. How do you respond?

A. Say that you thought that you had a good interview, and that you must have come up against somebody who happened to perform better than you did on the day.

B. Blame yourself for not having done sufficient preparation for the interview.

C. Pretend that you under-performed in the interview because you did not really want the job.

Scoring your answers

For each of Tests 1–4 compare your answers with those given in the keys below. For each item put a ring round your answer. The totals will be the number of answers you have ringed in each column.

Test 1	Most EI	Least EI	Intermediate
Item 1	A	C	B
2	A	B	C
3	B	A	C
4	A	B	C
5	C	A	B
6	B	A	C
Totals			

Test 2	Most EI	Least EI	Intermediate
Item 1	C	B	A
2	A	B	C
3	A	C	B
4	C	B	A
5	A	C	B
6	C	B	A
Totals			

Test 3	Most EI	Least EI	Intermediate
Item 1	C	B	A
2	B	A	C
3	B	A	C
4	B	A	C
5	A	C	B
6	A	B	C
Totals			

Test 4	Most EI	Least EI	Intermediate
Item 1	C	B	A
2	C	B	A
3	A	B	C
4	B	A	C
5	A	C	B
6	A	C	B
Totals			

Empathy

Empathy is the capacity to enter into someone else's mind and personality, and by so doing imaginatively experience that person's subjective feelings or inner emotions. It includes the ability to apply those skills and attributes at group and organizational levels, as well as person to person. Empathy is the means, therefore, by which we become aware of implicit signals, or 'emotional clues', that might otherwise have gone undetected. In effect, it is a highly sophisticated in-built sensing system – our 'social antennae'.

Getting the message: trusting our senses

We pick up covert signals from other people through observing their behaviour – the things they say and don't say, when they speak and when they remain silent, whom they speak to and how, whom they associate with and whom they ignore, their gestures and eye movements and mannerisms (all of which we call 'body language'), and the subtle changes in mood over time and in different contexts. In fact, a high proportion of the emotional messages we receive are non-verbal, which is why we stressed their importance as an element of self-awareness (see Chapter 3). As often as not, it is the anger in a person's tone of voice, the look in their eyes and the wagging of the finger, which tells us how they are truly feeling, rather than what they actually say. They might have controlled themselves better, but their behaviour has revealed important information about how they are feeling.

You might say that we count on other people to reveal themselves by an injudicious show of emotion, but there is more to empathy than what our five senses distinguish. The intuitive part of our minds – our extra-sensory perception or 'sixth sense' – picks up things that our other senses fail to recognize. Sometimes you just 'know' something without necessarily knowing how or why. You know that so-and-so will burst into tears, or that someone else will make an excuse and leave the room. For much of the time we seem to make no conscious effort even to notice, let alone pay attention to or try to make sense of, the masses of data we are assimilating. It is as if we are simply acting as a sponge, soaking it all up and storing it away deep beneath the surface for no apparent purpose other than for future reference should the need arise. In effect, you know but don't know that you know.

That said, our minds have a habit of going on working at a sub-conscious level – even when we are sleeping – and in so doing often create order out of randomly gathered and apparently disconnected fragments of verbal and non-verbal information. Then, as if by chance, something that a person does or says acts as a catalyst, and the pieces of the jigsaw begin to fall into place – that sense we had that something was wrong but we did not know what suddenly crystallizes and becomes apparent to us. Armed with these new emotional insights, we can begin to make subtle adjustments to our behaviour in order to accommodate them – a process known as 'attunement'.

What it means is this. If we are to behave in an emotionally intelligent manner, empathy needs to operate at three interdependent levels. At the lowest level is the primary sensing of the signals that people give out, which provide us with clues as to their inner emotions. These signals enable us to discern, without being told, the socio-political undercurrents that exist in groups and organizations – who the 'opinion leaders' are, who really makes the decisions, who the 'friends' and the 'enemies' are, and what are the tacit, unstated values and beliefs. If, for whatever reason, we are insensitive to these signs and fail to recognize them – if our 'social antennae' fail to work – we are deprived of the 'emotional clues' we need to inform our behaviour.

The consequences of misreading people should not be lightly dismissed. After all, we will be telling them something about ourselves – about our empathy or lack of it – and they in turn will begin to slap labels on us based on how they perceive our personality and behaviour.

Are you 'warm' or 'cold'?

In our everyday speech we frequently use words to describe people whose behavioural characteristics we associate with empathy or the lack of it: antipathy. For example, we might refer to someone who displays the former as being 'warm-hearted' or the latter as 'a cold fish'.

Take a look at the following list of words commonly used to describe the personal attributes of individuals we associate with having empathy: caring; sensitive; sympathetic; interested; feeling; friendly; understanding; good listener; people-centred. Add any others you can think of.

Now compile a matching set of words that convey the opposite meanings, and that when applied to a person would convey to you a lack of empathy. If you are stuck for ideas, try using the thesaurus on the word-processing program on your computer, which should give you lists of synonyms (words with the same meaning) and antonyms (words with the opposite meaning).

Arrange the words in your lists in pairs like 'cold' and 'warm' as points at either end of a five-point scale (see below).

Cold	1	2	3	4	5	Warm
	1	2	3	4	5	
	1	2	3	4	5	
	1	2	3	4	5	

Now is the time to do some self-evaluation. For each pair of words in your list, put a cross through the number that corresponds with your self-assessment. Once you have finished, get someone who knows you well to discuss your self-evaluation with you.

When we are open and receptive to emotional signals and social and political undercurrents we have to do much more than simply store them away. If they are to be really useful to us and to others, we must try to appreciate the standpoints of the individuals, groups and organizations from which they have emanated. This often requires no more than an act of imagination on our part, an attempt to sense what it would feel like to be in someone else's shoes when faced with a particular situation, or what it can be that is causing a group to behave in a certain way, such as agreeing to do one thing and then doing another. This can involve all or some of the following:

- talking to someone who knows a person better than we do;
- asking questions of somebody who has more experience of working with a particular group than we have;

■ studying the background material on an unfamiliar organization.

What this checking exercise does is enable us to triangulate our own perceptions against those of other people in the light of the additional data we have collected. It also helps us to put the people and situations we are considering into their broader contexts and in so doing inform our responses to them.

Above all, we have to use our sensitivity to the emotional clues we have picked up and our appreciation of the perspectives that produced them, to fine-tune our own actions so that we behave in emotionally intelligent ways. To do this well we need to be aware of our personal feelings (self-awareness) and be able to regulate our own emotional behaviour (self-regulation). It is no good being able to detect signs of someone else's inner turmoil, and to be able to view the situation from their perspective, if we are so unaware of our own emotional state, and so unable to regulate our reactions, that we behave in ways which are totally inappropriate. If that happens, we are likely to make matters worse, both for ourselves and the other people with whom we are involved.

Making a drama out of a crisis, or a crisis out of a drama?

Think about a situation you have observed, or to which you were a party, which started from something trivial, but escalated out of control. It could have been a quarrel between friends, a bitter argument in a meeting, or a disagreement at work. It could even be a dramatic scene from a television 'soap'. Write a short account of the chain of events as they unfolded, illustrated with examples of dialogue.

Then write a second scenario describing what might have happened had one or more of the parties concerned been capable of using empathy to good effect.

Aspects of empathy

You will recall that in Chapter 1 we broke down empathy into four key aspects:

- being sensitive towards and understanding other people;
- making the needs and interests of others your point of reference;
- furthering the development of other people;
- being socially and politically tuned in.

We will now discuss these in more detail. You will find a test associated with each one at the end of the chapter.

Being sensitive towards and understanding other people

Individuals with empathy are sensitive towards others and are willing to make the effort to understand their behaviour. This means that they not only are good at sensing other people's inner emotions, ie picking up sensory and extra-sensory clues about how others are feeling, but take time to try to understand their points of view. They don't just assume that another person feels the same way as they do and shares their perspective; they acknowledge that their own personal standpoint is not the only one worthy of consideration.

Take, for example, the speaker at an international conference in which the delegates (and the speaker) were receiving simultaneous translations of the proceedings into the language of their choice. At the end of the presentation the members of the audience were invited to express their own points of view on the issues under consideration and to put questions to the speaker. When one of the delegates spoke, she did so with an obvious passion that was at odds with the carefully modulated tones that the main speaker heard when the translator summarized what had been said. Instead of responding to the question posed by the delegate, the speaker opted to deal first with the emotions, which had been evident in the tone of voice, facial expressions and hand gestures she had used while she was speaking, and the nodding of heads in agreement of those around her.

So, the speaker responded by saying that he had heard what had been said via the translator but had also been struck by how forcibly the views had been expressed. He went on to suggest that the feelings that underpinned the things that had been said appeared to be too important to be simply brushed aside – they should be the starting point of the discussion. This initiated a constructive dialogue among those present in which different value-positions were clarified, common ground was explored and the subject matter was examined at considerable depth. What could have been a confrontational argument became instead a genuine meeting of hearts and minds.

Empathy, therefore, does not end with reading other people's feelings and attempting to understand their points of view; it involves using those insights in ways that are helpful to yourself as well as being supportive of the individuals, groups and organizations with whom you are involved.

Making the needs and interests of others your point of reference

People who excel in this aspect of empathy not only are good at sensing the emotional feelings and needs of others, but are willing to make the effort to view actions, events and situations from points of view other than their own and to act accordingly. Therefore, they do not assume that other people automatically share their perspective but recognize that in any given situation there is more than one viewpoint that needs to be considered. People who do not share this breadth of vision and openness to alternative perspectives are apt to encounter problems of an emotional nature at a multiplicity of levels ranging from close personal relationships through to their social interactions with other people, including those with whom they work.

Failure to see things from another person's point of view often leads to difficulties in personal relationships with family and friends. If your thoughts and inner feelings are not taken into consideration when decisions are being made, what can start off as mild irritation can over time escalate to the point at which it contributes to the breakdown of a relationship. Such behaviour may be forgiven if it is done in isolation where normally there is respect for each other's feelings and points of view. However, if it is done repeatedly in an inconsiderate way, it is likely to become a source of deep resentment, especially if the behaviour is accompanied by a total disregard for the effects it is having on the other person in the relationship.

Self-centred?

Choose a person from your own experience whom you would describe as 'self-centred' – it could be someone with whom you have (or have had) a close personal relationship or from a social group or team of which you are a member. Now think about the following questions.

- How does that person's self-centredness manifest itself in his or her behaviour?
- In what situations is the person being self-centred most apparent?
- What are the consequences for that person's relationships with others?
- What would it take to make that person recognize and accept other people's points of view?
- What lessons do you think you can draw from reflecting on the behaviour of the person concerned?

Individuals who are insensitive to the inner emotions of others, and are unable and/or unwilling to consider points of view other than their own, can also create problems for the groups, teams and organizations of which they are members. In situations such as these in which effective group functioning and team working are important, those who are only interested in achieving goals that are important to them can have an adverse effect on both morale and efficiency. In effect they are saying 'my feelings are the only ones that matter to me and my needs must come first'. By contrast, the shared ethics that bind together the best groups and teams put the collective well-being above all else. For the whole to be greater than the sum of the parts, individuals must be prepared to align their personal interests with those of the group or team.

Clearly, if this aspect of empathy has the capacity to influence the quality of our interpersonal relationships and how effectively we function as members of groups and teams, it must have an impact on our performance in other situations, including the workplace. Its most obvious manifestation is the disharmony that the absence of empathy can cause in working groups within organizations. However, it can also operate in subtle and unobtrusive ways that can easily go undetected, but that nevertheless can have an adverse impact on job performance.

Take as an illustration two customers visiting two wine shops. In shop A the customers noticed that the shelves had been restocked with one of their favourite wines. They liked it so much that they had ordered a case (12 bottles) several weeks before. Despite several phone calls and a previous visit to the shop, the order had not been delivered. When they asked an assistant (who happened to be sitting behind the counter reading a magazine) how much of the wine they had in stock, and if they could expect delivery of their order, they were told that what was on the shelves was probably all the shop had and that 'we've got so many orders to deal with we've scrapped all the old ones'. Result: no sale and no repeat business, despite the quality of the product. Lack of empathy and a failure to meet an organization's 'customer care pledge' comes at a price!

Needless to say, the visit to shop B proved to be very different. In this case, the assistant, who was busy stacking shelves, sensed that the customers were having difficulty finding the wine for which they were searching. She stopped what she was doing and asked if she could help. With her assistance the wine was found and a conversation ensued about its merits, which resulted in much more than an addition to the sales figures. Because the assistant had been sensitive to the fact that the customers were in need of help, and had acted accordingly, she had entered into a personal relationship with them that had made the experience of shopping a positive one from their point of view, if not from hers – after all, she still had the shelves to fill when they had gone! But what it also did was to increase the chances of repeat business and customer loyalty.

Furthering the development of other people

Individuals with strength in this aspect of empathy are of crucial importance in all kinds of situations, notably where children of all ages are being cared for and taught and where people are being trained and educated. Then there is the work-place, where work-based learning is increasingly seen as the key to the ongoing improvement of the goods and services that organizations provide. In this context, therefore, empathy has a key role to play in the advancement of lifelong learning.

It is clear that you can't get far in helping others if you lack awareness of how inner emotional turmoil can influence the performance of individuals and groups. The fact that we talk about 'the shakes', 'exam nerves' and 'stage fright' indicates that we are conscious of the way in which that turmoil can affect the way we perform, whether it be in a driving test, an examination, a 'big game' (albeit at the local leisure centre), or the first day in a new job. Not that the relationship between our inner feelings and the quality of our performance is straight-forward. In some circumstances a degree of nervous edginess – being 'up for it' – is probably beneficial so long as it is kept under control. On the other hand, as we all know from experience, an excess of anxiety can have an adverse impact on how we perform, especially when we regard the stakes as particularly high. Remember those presentations and job interviews?

Butterflies

Try to identify situations in which your inner feelings (maybe 'butterflies in your stomach') had an impact on the way you performed. Reflect on the following questions.

- What made you feel the way that you did, and just exactly how did your feelings influence your performance?
- In what ways did the behaviour of other people influence how you felt?
- Are there any lessons you can draw from this, particularly with regard to how you treat other people when they are in similar situations?

Being sensitive to the subjective feelings others are experiencing, and appreciating the impact that these inner emotions can have on how they perform, is central to successful parenting, teaching, coaching, mentoring and managing. This sensitivity enables you to recognize, for example, that individuals can have emotional blocks that impede their development by preventing them from learning effectively or performing to the best of their ability. These include being afraid to make a mistake; fear of looking foolish in front of other people; a need for instant success leading to a feeling of impatience; an inability to cope with uncertainty, resulting in anxiety in situations that are not clear-cut; and nervousness in contexts associated with previous failure.

On the positive side, all of us can experience or generate feelings that can have a positive effect on our learning and performance. Consider the confidence you can get from tackling routine tasks; the deep sense of satisfaction gained from completing a project by yourself and in your own time, and the pleasure to be got from solving problems under pressure.

Being tuned in socially and politically

Go back to a time when you started a new job, or your first job. As soon as you set foot in the building you were no doubt struck by a number of features – perhaps the clothes people were wearing, the degree of formality of the interactions between people, the friendliness of the reception and security staff, the office furniture, the use of colour, the amount and nature of company literature available, and so on. These and numerous other features provided you with a set of clues as to how that organization was operating, what approaches worked there, and which ones were unlikely to work. What you were getting was your first insights into the unwritten and unspoken rules operating in that organization, those rules that the 'old hands' take for granted but which you must learn and apply if you are to survive and then prosper. It is this aspect of empathy we are talking about – being socially and politically tuned in to the situations in which you find yourself.

To be clued up is to be capable of detecting the informal social structures and hidden power relationships that are found within groups and organizations. Beneath what might seem like surface calm there are powerful currents and counter-currents that can be extremely treacherous to the unwary – that is to say, those who lack social and political awareness. Where are the undocumented alliances, friendship groups, cliques and power bases? The true insider knows exactly where power and influence reside and how they are exercised – who is supposed to be in charge and who really pulls the strings and makes all the key decisions. They also know who the 'opinion leaders' are – those people you need to convince first about the wisdom of a particular course of action if you are to have any chance of persuading the rest.

Insider knowledge

Think hard about a team, group or organization of which you are an established member.

Make a list of all the things about it that you think an outsider might be able to surmise.

Then make a list of those things about it that can only be learnt by becoming an insider.

Use your two lists to write a 'Rough Guide' for your group, team or organization aimed at helping a newcomer to survive.

Having an unerring feel for the rules of the game is even more important in those charged with the responsibility of managing and leading groups, teams and whole organizations. But, of course, in addition to social and political awareness, this also requires all of the other aspects of empathy we have identified: sensitivity to the subjective feelings of other people, a willingness to consider alternative points of view and the ability to further the development of others.

The tests

For every **item** in **each** of the tests choose **one** answer by circling option A, B or C. Remember, in the cause of accuracy of assessment, you should circle the action closest to what you would do, or have been doing. Do not opt for what you now think is the best or most admirable thing to do. After all, to want to put yourself in the most favourable light is hardly an emotionally intelligent way of responding. A key is provided at the end of the tests, which will enable you to score your answers.

Test 1

1. You notice that a member of your group who is usually bright and cheerful has become quiet and withdrawn. How do you respond?
A. Reason that the change in mood has nothing to do with you and that the person will probably revert to normal behaviour without any interference from you.
B. Ask other members of the group if someone will have a word.
C. Find an occasion to talk to the person one-to-one; voice your concerns about his or her well being and ask if there is anything you can do to help.

2. You are at a party. A close friend who has been quiet all evening suddenly breaks down in tears. How do you respond?
A. Go to the friend and offer 'tea and sympathy' away from the gaze of other people.
B. Tell the friend to stop making such a fuss as his or her behaviour is embarrassing you in front of other people.
C. Ignore the friend; move to another part of the room.

3. You and the others in your group are due to give an important presentation, and you observe that one of the group who is due to take a lead role is becoming extremely agitated. How do you respond?
A. Offer to change roles with the person concerned.
B. Open up a conversation with the person; say that you are beginning to feel the strain of the occasion and ask how he or she is coping.
C. Put it down to a case of 'stage fright' and disregard the signals you are getting.

4. You know that it is easy to 'wind up' a colleague if you press the right buttons when the time is right. The time seems to be right. How do you respond?

A. Succumb to the temptation to play to the crowd by winding up the colleague.

B. Having read the signs, try to take action such as distracting attention away from the person concerned in an attempt to defuse the situation.

C. Stand back and enjoy watching somebody else do the winding up for you.

5. You have a hunch that something is troubling someone who is close to you. How do you respond?

A. Trust your inner feelings and try to find a way of broaching the subject with the person concerned.

B. Wait for the person to say or do something first to confirm your suspicions, then act accordingly.

C. Dismiss your inner feelings and do nothing on the grounds that your hunch could be wrong.

6. Although nothing has been said exactly, you sense that for some reason you have offended a small group of your friends or colleagues. How do you respond?

A. Think back carefully over your actions to see if you can put your finger on what it might be that you have done to upset them.

B. Say to them that you sense that something is affecting your relationship with them and that you are sorry if it proves to be your fault. Ask if you can all talk about it.

C. Shrug the whole thing off reasoning that it's too late to do anything about it and it's their problem anyway.

Test 2

1. You have been asked to pass on to a colleague an unexpected piece of bad news of a personal nature. How do you respond?

A. Get it over with as soon as you can – find the colleague and come straight out with the bad news.

B. Put off doing it by trying to persuade somebody else to do it for you.
C. Find the person straight away and break the news as gently as possible, and then provide what support you can.

2. You receive a text message inviting you and a close friend who is not with you at the time to go out for the evening. How do you respond?
A. Send an immediate message back saying that you will give them a definite answer as soon as you have contacted your friend.
B. Reply immediately saying that you will definitely go and that your friend may or may not be with you.
C. Send a message back straight away saying that both you and your friend are glad to accept the invitation.

3. You have worked hard on a project that is near completion and a colleague suggests that it would have been better had you done it differently. How do you respond?
A. Tell your colleague not to interfere with something for which you have responsibility.
B. Listen politely to what the person has to say and then complete the project as you originally intended.
C. Listen carefully to what the person has to say and then re-examine your plans for the completion of the project, making such changes as you consider necessary.

4. At the last minute you are offered a single ticket for an event you have been longing to attend. If you accept, it will mean cancelling a commitment you have made to attend a party for a close friend. How do you respond?
A. Turn down the offer, but make sure that your friend knows how noble you have been not to cancel at short notice.
B. Don't hesitate – accept the ticket and go to the event.
C. Turn down the offer and attend the party without saying anything about the event.

5. You are out clothes-shopping with a new friend who keeps on buying garments that you think are very unflattering. How do you respond?
A. Ask your friend if they would mind if you suggested some alternative items of clothing to consider.
B. Don't interfere, reasoning that it is no concern of yours what your friend chooses to buy.
C. Tell the friend in no uncertain terms how awful you think the clothes look.

6. You are in a public place where other people are sitting talking or quietly reading newspapers or magazines and you receive a call on your mobile. How do you respond?
A. Switch off the dial tone and move to a place where you can deal with the call without disturbing other people.
B. Deal with the call as if you were on your own in private and leave the mobile switched on to receive incoming calls when you have finished.
C. Deal with the call as you normally would and then shut off your mobile.

Test 3

1. Some members of your team are performing below their potential and below what is needed if the team is to be successful. How do you respond?
A. Seek every opportunity to praise their efforts.
B. Reason that they will know that they are not performing to the standard required and will do something about it themselves.
C. Find an occasion to discuss the contribution they are making to the team and encourage them to set themselves new goals.

2. You observe a colleague handling a situation badly and you are worried about the consequences. How do you respond?

A. Intervene and take immediate responsibility for the situation, while saying little by way of explanation to the person concerned.

B. Do nothing at the time, but resolve to do your best to pick up the pieces as soon as possible.

C. Make your presence known to all concerned and ask if you can assist your colleague in any way. Discuss the lessons that can be learnt from the way you both handled the situation.

3. As part of a training exercise a member of your team has given a presentation and it is your job to provide some one-to-one feedback. How do you respond?

A. Ask the person to evaluate their own performance, offering your own comments and observations as and when appropriate.

B. Concentrate on highlighting the good things you noted.

C. Try to give a rounded set of comments about the presentation by balancing praise with criticism.

4. You have been given a piece of work that you consider to be seriously sub-standard. How do you respond?

A. Hand it back and demand that it be redone as soon as possible, adding that this is the last chance to get it right.

B. Make a note of all the errors and weaknesses and go through those with the person concerned before they correct the piece of work.

C. Invite the person to do a self-evaluation of the piece of work and then discuss it with the person, providing feedback as and when appropriate and concluding with an agreed list of action points.

5. Someone at an adjacent workstation is having difficulty coping with the new computer software, thus holding up the work of the team. How do you respond?

A. Give verbal instructions to the person concerned as to how he or she should proceed and then get on with your own work.

B. Recognize the importance of the task to the team; drop what you are doing immediately; take over the job and do it yourself.
C. Ask the person to explain what it is that is causing the problem and then sit beside them for a short time while he or she works, providing coaching as and when appropriate.

6. A colleague has made a big effort to organize an event that proved to be highly successful. You had no chance to congratulate the person before you left. How do you respond?
A. Assume that other people will have voiced their appreciation and offered their congratulations.
B. Make a mental note to say 'Thanks and well done' next time you meet.
C. Send an e-mail to your colleague as soon as you can, praising his or her efforts.

Test 4

1. As you approach a small group of people you hardly know, they stop talking to each other just as you are about to join them. How do you respond?
A. Jokingly accuse them of talking about somebody behind their back – possibly you – and see how they respond.
B. Carry on as if you hadn't noticed anything unusual about their behaviour.
C. Assume that they were having a private conversation, apologize for interrupting, and ask if it's all right for you to join them.

2. You are due to visit a club or organization you have never visited before and someone who knows it well offers to tell you 'all there is to know about it'. How do you respond?
A. Turn down the offer on the grounds that it will be better to find out for yourself at first hand.

B. Accept the offer, but keep an open mind on what the person has to say until you have had a chance to compare it with information from other sources.

C. Reluctantly accept the offer, but view with deep distrust everything the person says.

3. You find that for no apparent reason a group that you have just joined is turning down all your ideas. How do you respond?

A. Stop coming up with new ideas, reasoning, 'Why waste my time?'

B. Try to come up with even better ideas than before.

C. Try to think of ways in which you can gain support for your ideas with influential individuals within the group.

4. You have recently joined a new organization and keep running into unexpected difficulties over how things should be done even though you have followed 'official' procedures. How do you respond?

A. Experiment with doing things your own way based on your own previous experience.

B. Seek out advice from colleagues with a reputation within the organization for 'getting things done'.

C. Continue to 'go by the book' and be prepared to put up with the frustration.

5. You have joined a group or organization because you were attracted by its policy on equal treatment for its members, but in reality find that it is not strictly applied in all cases. How do you respond?

A. As a matter of principle, resign from the group or organization as soon as you can, telling everybody why you are leaving.

B. Make sure that you personally behave in ways that comply with the official policy on this matter and draw the attention of the 'powers that be' to the mismatch between policy and practice.

C. Live with the situation, arguing that if people are unhappy at the way they are being treated, they can either complain or resign.

6. You have been invited to join a group that can help your career. Outwardly the group seems to be warm and friendly but you sense that beneath the surface this may not be the case. How do you respond?
A. Take the group at face value – assume that these people are as warm and friendly as they appear to be.
B. Tell yourself that it does not matter what the others are really like because you are going to look after your own interests.
C. Proceed with caution, giving yourself time to find out more about the friendship patterns within the group.

Scoring your answers

For each of Tests 1–4 compare your answers with those given in the keys below. For each item put a ring round your answer. The totals will be the number of answers you have ringed in each column.

Test 1	Most EI	Least EI	Intermediate
Item 1	C	B	A
2	A	B	C
3	B	C	A
4	B	A	C
5	A	C	B
6	B	C	A
Totals			

Test 2	Most EI	Least EI	Intermediate
Item 1	C	A	B
2	A	C	B
3	C	A	B
4	C	B	A
5	A	C	B
6	A	B	C
Totals			

Test 3	Most EI	Least EI	Intermediate
Item 1	C	B	A
2	C	A	B
3	A	B	C
4	C	A	B
5	C	B	A
6	C	B	A
Totals			

Test 4	Most EI	Least EI	Intermediate
Item 1	C	B	A
2	B	A	C
3	C	A	B
4	B	C	A
5	B	A	C
6	C	B	A
Totals			

Social skills

Social skills are an important component within the complex system of interrelated competencies that we call EI. It is our social skills that enable us to do such things as initiate and sustain personal relationships; become accepted and integrated into groups; function effectively as members of teams; influence the attitudes, opinions and behaviour of others; lead other people, including in some cases whole organizations, and prevent conflicts from happening – or at least manage them successfully when they do occur.

Relating to others

'No man is an island, entire of itself.' (John Donne) Social skills, therefore, are important in all aspects of our lives – unless of course you are living as a recluse on a desert island in total isolation from other people. However, for the majority of us, the possession of 'people skills' is an essential requirement for the conduct of our lives as active members of society, including what we do in our leisure time and at work. Employers have woken up to this. Increasingly, they are looking for people who possess not just the technical competence needed to accomplish tasks in the workplace but also – and, perhaps above all else – 'people' or 'soft' skills. What are these skills? They are no less than the ability to communicate, and the ability to work effectively and harmoniously with others.

Situations vacant

Take a close look at the 'Situations vacant' columns of a broadsheet newspaper. For each of the major job classifications make a list of the skills that the employers have identified and then answer the following questions:

- Where do social skills feature in these requirements?
- Are social skills needed in some types of employment more than they are in others?
- Which skills, if any, are needed across all of the occupational sectors?

The changes in the skills requirements of employers reflect, of course, the shift in the economy away from manufacturing to services and to knowledge-based forms of employment. Paradoxically, new technology, which has helped to drive many of these changes, is also making it possible for more and more people to work from home in relative isolation from their colleagues. While some individuals undoubtedly enjoy the flexibility that home working brings to their lives, others miss the daily face-to-face interactions with their workmates – e-mails and phone calls being a poor substitute for chats round the drinks machine and socializing after work. Nevertheless, if you happen to be working at home, your interpersonal skills will continue to come into play whenever you answer the telephone, and your communication skills (or lack of them) will be in evidence even in your text messages – well, to some extent, anyway.

Social skills and the other components of EI

Although it is convenient to discuss them under a separate heading, it is worth remembering that social skills do not function in isolation from the other components of emotional intelligence. For example, if we are to respond appropriately to other people, either as individuals or in groups, we need to draw upon our powers of empathy (see Chapter 5) in order to sense how they are feeling and imagine how things appear from their point of view. In other words, our 'social antennae' need to be fully operational so that we can detect the verbal and non-verbal signals that others are sending out concerning their inner feelings or emotional states. This is difficult enough at times in situations with which we are familiar and with people we know well, but it becomes even more problematic when we are in unfamiliar circumstances and in the company of strangers.

The problem is exacerbated when we find ourselves in situations in which we are in contact with people who are different from ourselves. For example, depending on our own upbringing and life experiences, we may find it more or less difficult to deploy our social skills to good effect in contexts in which the people we encounter differ from us by age, education, ethnicity, gender, nationality, religion and/or socio-economic background. In such circumstances communication in its widest sense can be fraught with difficulties. This is not just because of differences in our use of English but because of subtle cultural differences and nuances in our non-verbal communication or body language. Since these are an important means by which we send and receive messages concerning our inner feelings, there is a danger that we may seriously misinterpret what others are really 'saying', and vice versa. Consequently, in cases where cross-cultural communication is involved we need to be willing to question our assumptions and to listen attentively to what people are saying and watch carefully how they are behaving in order to fine-tune our responses to them. We must also be prepared to question the accuracy of the ways in which we are 'reading' the speech and behaviour of other people, and conversely how they are interpreting what we are saying and doing.

All alone in a crowd

Talk to various people you know about their experience of being in a minority within a group. This can be because of age, education, ethnicity, gender, nationality, occupation, religion, socio-economic background or even being left-handed as opposed to right-handed. In particular you might ask them:

- what it felt like to be in a minority;
- how being in a minority affected how other people treated them;
- what strategies they adopted for coping with such situations.

Finally, give some thought to what lessons you can learn from their experiences.

Because what matters is not just what we say but how we say it, including use of all of those non-verbal signals, the chances are that others will immediately recognize any inconsistencies between what we are saying and what we are truly feeling. We might well be saying how sorry or glad we are at someone's news, but we have to be able to communicate the sincerity of those words by our whole demeanour – as the Eagles song says, 'You can't hide those lyin' eyes'. In effect, there has to be consistency between our body language and what we are saying – and hence what is truly in our hearts and minds. This, of course, requires a good deal of self-regulation (see Chapter 2) as well as self-awareness (see Chapter 3).

Meeting new people, developing relationships, building networks, becoming a valued member of social groups, working effectively in teams, and influencing and leading others all require a lot of effort and commitment, and strength in that other component of EI: motivation (see Chapter 4). Social skills might appear to come easily to some people, but that often hides the amount of time, effort and attention to detail that they put into building and maintaining their relationships, working with others and developing their leadership skills. The old adage that 'you get as much out as you put in' can be applied every bit as much to our personal relationships, membership of social groups and working within teams as it does to any other aspect of our lives, including acquiring qualifications and building our careers. Given the importance that employers now attach to the possession of social skills, the development of your competence in this component of EI may be one of the keys to advancing your career.

Aspects of social skills

You will recall that in Chapter 1 we broke social skills down into three major aspects as follows:

- developing and sustaining interpersonal relationships;
- communicating with others;
- working with others.

We will now discuss these in more detail. You will find a test associated with each one at the end of the chapter.

Developing and sustaining relationships

People who are good at this aspect of social skills tend to have a number of behavioural characteristics in common. Fortunately, there is no secret about what these are – they are in fact well known and there is nothing to stop you from learning them. But doing that is not quite as simple as it sounds. When you are meeting people face to face for the first time and initiating relationships with them, the 'basics' seem to be good eye contact, smiling, positive body language, standing close but not so close as to invade their private space – four feet away from someone at a social gathering as a 'rule of thumb' – and even a touch of flattery. But these rules cannot be applied mechanistically; you have to be prepared to vary them according to the context. For example, maintaining eye contact for too long can easily be interpreted as a stare and make someone feel uncomfortable; likewise, too much flattery can smack of insincerity. In order to make the rules work, therefore, you need to put into practice components of EI such as your self-awareness, empathy and sensitivity to all the codes and signals of interpersonal communication.

It is possible that you have the social skills needed to initiate personal relationships, but lack the opportunity to do so. For example, most of our friendships originate out of regular contact that we have with other people at school, college, work, clubs and societies. However, your circumstances may be such that some or all of these opportunities for making face-to-face contacts and building up social networks are not open to you, perhaps because you work from home or have family commitments that restrict your freedom of action. That said, new technology enables us to both 'get in touch' and 'keep in touch' with people remotely, eg through Internet 'chat rooms' and by mobile phone.

Networking

Your network is simply a way of describing the people you know and how they are connected to you. Here are some questions to help you think about your personal networks.

- How would you categorize the people with whom you have a personal relationship (eg family, neighbours, people you know through your family, school/college friends, colleagues from work, leisure interests, people from the UK or abroad)?
- Do you have a range of personal networks or are they restricted to just a few (eg family, school friends or colleagues)?
- Do you have a mixture of old and new relationships?
- Are you adding new ones to your list?
- Do you have both informal networks (eg family and friends) and formal networks (eg through membership of a society or a professional association)?

Now that you have thought about your personal networks and how you acquired them, are there any actions you think you should take? It might be to revive an old relationship or even let go of one or two.

Although the business of initiating personal relationships and establishing networks requires both social skills and the presence of opportunities, maintaining them demands both skill and commitment. While some of our friends and social contacts can be described as being 'low maintenance' because they are easy to sustain, others definitely fall into the 'high maintenance' category. Long-term 'best friends' who are always 'there for us' when we need their support, but who are undemanding of us in terms of both time and attention, belong in the former group. At the other end of the spectrum there are those people who take up a lot of our time, demand our attention and often leave us feeling tired, frustrated and at times emotionally drained. It is worth giving some thought, therefore, to the roles that different people play in our lives and the emotional impact that they have on us (and indeed that we have on them).

What's a friend for?

Unlike family members, friends have no obvious rules and obligations to observe and discharge. The absence of these boundaries can make for strong bonds, but also for fraught times when pressures bend the relationship. Here are some questions to help you to think through the roles that different people play in your life and the emotional impact that they have on you, and you have on them.

- Who are the people who are there to support you when the going gets tough?
  - What forms does their support take?
  - What do they get out of their relationship with you?
  - How are these relationships maintained?
- Who are the people you are 'there for' in similar circumstances?
  - What forms does your support take?
  - What do you get out of your relationship with these people?
  - How are these relationships maintained?
- Who are the people who take up too much of your time and drain your energy?
- Who are the people who inspire you and give you energy, for example by acting as your role models?
  - What is it about these people that you admire?
- Who are your mentors – the people who help you to grow?
  - How are these relationships maintained?
- Who are the people you help and encourage?
  - How are these relationships maintained?

- Who are the people (if any) whom you regard as your 'enemies'?
  - How is their opposition manifested; for example, are they opposed to you or your ideas?
  - What impact does their opposition have on you?

Now that you have reflected on these matters, are there any actions that you think you should now take?

Communicating with others

Communicating is about conveying information, ideas and feelings to one another. We do this for a whole variety of reasons: to increase other people's knowledge and understanding or to influence their attitudes and/or behaviour. Unfortunately, communication is often undervalued, taken for granted even; we make an assumption that other people know, or already know, or will work it out for themselves, or actually don't need to know. Or perhaps we just think that it is not worth passing information on to them. We behave as if communication is optional, which is a dangerous way of proceeding. The borrowing from the military of the notion of sharing information on a 'need to know' basis has not helped. In the survey of 500 senior UK managers mentioned in Chapter 1, nearly three out of ten stated that they won't open up to their team – considering it wholly inappropriate to take staff into their confidence. That survey pinpointed poor communication skills as central to managerial incompetence.

Unwillingness or reluctance to communicate also illustrates a certain lack of empathy. In effect, you are overlooking or failing to imagine how the other person or, conceivably, institution might benefit from the communication you are withholding. In the wake of the terrorist attacks in the United States on 11 September 2001, it became very clear that the various law enforcement agencies round the world had been lax in their duty to share vital information with each other. Certainly, there are challenges in communicating across cultures (and we come on to those shortly) but those challenges are there to be met, not thrown aside.

It is clear that, to be effective, communication has to be a two-way process. You are not just the encoder and transmitter of messages to other people, but also the target for other people's messages. Accordingly, you have to pay attention if you are to receive and decode correctly the various communications they are sending in your direction. That is why we talk about 'Chinese whispers' – what happens when a message is progressively degraded as it passes from one person to another. (By such process what starts off as 'We had a new car' can end up as 'We ate a brand new car'.)

Precisely because it is a 'two-way street', communication is not just about telling people things; it's also about listening and looking, if you wish to interpret correctly what it is that they are trying to say to you in return. To complicate matters, we are almost certainly not all talking the same language. It has been estimated that in the UK only 3 per cent of the population speak what is known as 'Received Standard English' – the formal speech sometimes known as 'BBC English'.

Divided by a common language

It was George Bernard Shaw who quipped that the British and the Americans are 'divided by a common language'. In so doing, he was drawing attention to the diversity of styles within the English language.

The quip highlights the role of cultural differences in communication. In order to get some personal insights into this aspect of social skills, talk to various people you know about their experiences of 'cross-cultural communication' (eg as a result of differences in age, education, ethnicity, first language, gender, nationality, occupation and socio-economic background). You might ask them about:

- verbal communication;
- non-verbal communication;
- particular difficulties they encountered;
- what strategies they adopted for coping with those difficulties.

Finally, give some thought to what lessons you can learn from their experiences.

Misunderstandings readily arise from making easy assumptions about sharing a 'common language', not least because modern society is pluralistic. Consequently, despite the prevalence of the use of English (though not necessarily for some as their first language), we need to be able to communicate effectively through it in contexts that are culturally diverse. In order to do so we need to question our own cultural assumptions and in so doing take into account the ways in which differences in, for example, education, ethnicity, gender, social background and experience can lead to variations in the following:

- tone of voice and patterns of stress (eg to manage the flow of information, clarify meaning and to express emotions);
- pattern of 'taking turns' in conversation (eg disruption of the familiar flow of dialogue can be a source of irritation);
- ways of expressing agreement and disagreement (eg when someone says 'Yes' this could mean 'I've heard you' and not 'I agree with you');
- codes and conventions used for signalling politeness;
- ways of structuring arguments and information;
- how emotions are expressed, including the extent to which it is considered appropriate to express emotions in a particular context.

It should be easy to see, therefore, why misunderstandings can arise when people from different 'speech communities' try to talk to each other, especially if each person uses his or her own cultural framework to interpret what the others are saying. The emotionally intelligent response to such situations is to try to manage the interactions effectively, especially your contribution to them. It is unhelpful to blame the other person(s) for any breakdown in communications.

Working with others

Competence in working with others is an important aspect of the social skills component of EI. It is much sought-after by employers but it has wider significance outside the world of work. Families, clubs, societies and teams all require people who are capable of working effectively with each other – individuals who are 'good team players'. That does not mean to say that they all have to like each other or have similar character-istics – quite the opposite, because teams often require a mixture of members with individual skills, abilities and person-alities. However, what they do need in common is a willingness to collaborate with each other in pursuit of agreed goals. Yet mutual goodwill and a readiness to cooperate with each other are not enough; groups, teams and organizations require people who are skilled at working with others.

So what are the skills we need if we are to work effectively with other people? At the surface level, what groups (both large and small) need are individuals who are capable of meeting their own responsibilities within an agreed organizational framework. Yet even that is only part of the picture, because if groups and even whole organizations are to function efficiently and harmoniously, they require people who can fulfil unspec-ified roles that they take upon themselves. These are the indi-viduals who make a contribution to the common good over and above that which they achieve just by doing their job. They are the ones who have the ability to cheer people up when they are feeling down, sense when they are feeling tired, cajole indi-viduals into action and make the whole greater than the sum of the parts.

Team players

With regard to a group, team or organization of which you are a member, think about the roles that different people play. As you are doing this make notes under the following headings:

Person (name)

Ascribed ('official') role(s)

Assumed ('unofficial') role(s)

How the person fulfils his or her role including the skills he or she uses.

What lessons can you learn from the above analysis about this aspect of the social skills component of emotional intelligence?

The tests

For every **item** in each of the **tests** choose **one** answer by circling option A, B or C. Remember, in the cause of accuracy of assessment, you should circle the action closest to what you would do, or have been doing. Do not opt for what you now think is the best or most admirable thing to do. After all, to want to put yourself in the most favourable light is hardly an emotionally intelligent way of responding. A key is provided at the end of the tests which will enable you to score your answers.

Test 1

1. You suspect that someone close to you is unhappy about something you have done, but when you ask how he or she felt about it, the person simply said 'OK'. How do you respond?

A. Take what was said at face value – that everything really is OK.
B. Wait until you think the time is right and then encourage the person to open up and talk about how he or she truly feels.
C. Assume that the person would rather not talk to you about it – respect the 'right to silence' on this matter.

2. You arrive at a party and contrary to your expectations you find that you know very few people. How do you respond?
A. Head straight for the few people you know in the hope that they'll introduce you to some of the other guests.
B. Let your host and your friends know that you have arrived, and then 'take the plunge' by introducing yourself to some of the other guests.
C. Stay for a little while, making sure that you at least talk to your host.

3. It is some time since you had any contact with one of your friends. How do you respond?
A. Take the initiative and get in touch with the friend to ask how he or she is getting on.
B. Reason that, like you, the person has probably been busy and will get in touch with you in his or her own good time.
C. Assume that the person has found new friends and don't expect to hear from him or her.

4. You are introduced to someone who seems to be nervous and hesitant about engaging in conversation. How do you respond?
A. Pretend to listen and take an interest in what the person is trying to say before moving off to talk to somebody else.
B. Listen carefully to what the person is saying, don't interrupt and when you do speak, try to respond positively to what the person has said.
C. Take advantage of the first pause in the conversation to start talking yourself.

5. You have just made friends with someone who is new to the area in which you live. How do you respond?
A. Introduce the person to your friends, but only when you are forced to do so.
B. Use every opportunity to introduce the person to your network of friends and social contacts.
C. Allow the person to settle in and to develop other friendships him- or herself.

6. A friend has run into a serious problem and is in urgent need of your help. To offer that help would cause you a great deal of inconvenience. How do you respond?
A. Agree to help, but only if no one else can be found.
B. Recognize the seriousness of the person's predicament and offer your support.
C. Point out the inconvenience it would cause you and suggest that the person tries someone else.

Test 2

1. You are in conversation with someone who is trying to explain something to you but is taking a long time about it and you have important things to do. How do you respond?
A. Make any excuse you can think of to bring the conversation to an end.
B. Explain to the person that you have pressing things to do and ask him or her to sum up the main points in the argument.
C. Say nothing, but make a point of looking at your watch.

2. A colleague is talking to you about a complex issue, but you are having difficulty in concentrating on what they are saying. How do you respond?
A. Try to give the impression that you are listening and wait until the ordeal is over.
B. Suppress a yawn, say that you are very tired, and ask if you can talk about it some other time.
C. Keep asking questions until you have developed an understanding of what the person is saying.

3. You are in conversation with someone and your eyes seem to be telling you something different from what your ears are hearing. How do you respond?
A. Say as politely as you can that you are unclear about what is being said and seek clarification about the matters that concern you.
B. Treat with suspicion what is being said but make a mental note to check it out later.
C. Shrug off your doubts and take what is being said at its face value.

4. You have left a series of messages on a person's answer-phone saying that you need to speak urgently, but he or she has not returned your calls. How do you respond?
A. Check up to see if anyone knows why the person might not be responding to your calls, and if there doesn't seem to be a problem, try again.
B. Leave another message on the answerphone voicing your frustration.
C. Try to contact the person again, but this time using as many different methods as are available to you.

5. You are talking to someone over the 'phone and you detect from the pauses and tone of voice that the person you are speaking to may be deliberately holding something back. How do you respond?
A. Let the person know that you think that he or she is trying to deceive you.
B. Distrust what was said and try to find out from other sources what the person might have been holding back.
C. Sum up what you think the person has said and ask directly if there is anything else he or she wants to tell you or that you should know.

6. A newcomer to your group is having difficulty under-standing its 'jargon' and 'in-jokes'. How do you respond?
A. Carry on as usual – it's up to the newcomer to adapt to the group and not the other way about.

B. Correct the newcomer's misunderstandings whenever they occur.
C. Find time to explain some of the 'jargon' and 'in-jokes' to the newcomer and encourage others to do the same.

Test 3

1. You begin to sense that too many jokes are being made at the expense of a good-natured member of your team, and that the person concerned has had enough of being treated in this way. How do you respond?
A. Have a quiet word with each of your colleagues to voice your concerns over the way they are treating their team-mate and suggest that they change their behaviour.
B. Try to deflect the humour away from the person concerned towards other members of the team.
C. Do nothing – wait for the other members of the team to get the message and stop what they are doing.

2. A number of minor setbacks in quick succession have left everyone in your team feeling depressed and dispirited. How do you respond?
A. Keep smiling, adopt a positive and optimistic attitude, and try to get your team-mates to put the setbacks into perspective.
B. Give the team a 'good talking to' by telling them to grow up and pull themselves together.
C. Do nothing – just wait for everybody to get over it in his or her own good time.

3. Members of your group normally get on with each other extremely well, then suddenly they start to bicker among themselves for no apparent reason. How do you respond?
A. Encourage people to bring their 'hidden agendas' out into the open in an attempt to clear the air and get relationships back to normal.
B. Join in the bickering – take advantage of the opportunity to get a few things off your chest about one or two of your colleagues.

C. Try to avoid making matters worse – keep yourself to yourself and when you do speak take care not to give people any ammunition they can use against you.

4. You have had a team meeting and everyone has agreed to do things in the same way. Two people in the team then proceed to ignore the decision and 'do their own thing'. How do you respond?
A. Allow the rest of the team some time to put pressure on them to conform.
B. Confront them with the evidence and question their integrity.
C. Request a meeting at which the matter and its implications are discussed by the whole team.

5. A normally reliable member of your team arrives late and is clearly agitated over something. How do you respond?
A. Allow the incident to pass without comment.
B. Demand an immediate apology to the rest of the team followed by an explanation.
C. Ask if the person needs some time to him- or herself and offer your support if it is needed.

6. A member of your group is a perfectionist who worries about small things. He or she has refused all offers of help to get an urgent job done on time. How do you respond?
A. Remind the person of the consequences of continuing to refuse offers of help and ask how he or she proposes to get the job done on time.
B. Tell the person that he or she is letting the group down by refusing offers of help.
C. Get the group together, including the person concerned, to agree the best course of action.

Scoring your answers

For each of Tests 1–3 compare your answers with those given in the keys below. For each item put a ring round your answer. The totals will be the number of answers you have ringed in each column.

Test 1	Most EI	Least EI	Intermediate
Item 1	B	A	C
2	B	C	A
3	A	C	B
4	B	A	C
5	B	C	A
6	B	C	A
Totals			

Test 2	Most EI	Least EI	Intermediate
Item 1	B	A	C
2	C	B	A
3	A	C	B
4	C	B	A
5	C	A	B
6	C	A	B
Totals			

Test 3	Most EI	Least EI	Intermediate
Item 1	A	C	B
2	A	C	B
3	A	B	C
4	C	B	A
5	C	B	A
6	C	B	A
Totals			

7

Scoring, interpretation, reflection and a postscript

Now is the time to summarize and reflect on the results that have emerged from the exercises and tests you have completed. What you should get from the statistics produced by the analysis of the tests is an indication of the make-up of your emotional intelligence, including pointers to the distribution of your strengths and weaknesses. Think of it as an emotional 'health check'. By all means take it seriously, but don't take the outcomes so much to heart that they disturb your equilibrium. If you allow yourself get upset, then it is likely that you are being too self-critical – which, as we explained earlier, is not an emotionally intelligent response.

The chances are that the analysis will identify and confirm areas of your EI where, through your own self-knowledge and feedback from others, you already know you need to improve. Where the analysis helps you to identify something that has never occurred to you before, check it out with someone whose judgement you trust. The same applies to anything that puzzles you, which you are inclined to dismiss, as 'That cannot possibly be me!' Finally, what you must avoid is saying to yourself, 'Yeah, yeah, tell me something new. I'm no saint, but then who is?' If you approach self-reflection with such an attitude, then you have probably been wasting your time working your way through this book. While we accept that at times some of the most EI options in the test items can appear to verge on the saintly, the point is that they represent behaviour towards which you should aspire if your aim is to improve your EI.

Let us start the analysis by taking a closer look at how your answers are distributed by identifying how many most emotionally intelligent responses you produced (called 'Most EI' in the scoring key); how many least emotionally intelligent responses (called 'Least EI'); and how many of the rest (called 'Intermediate'). To that end, please go back to the last page of each of Chapters 2–6 to retrieve the numbers you recorded in each category. Use the boxes given below to make a note of those figures and the totals.

Once you have done that, take some time to study the distributions you have produced. Use the spaces provided in each box to write down comments about your scores on particular tests, and how they are distributed across all of the tests. There are boxes later in the chapter to help you pull everything together, and arrive at some conclusions.

Self-regulation	Most EI	Least EI	Intermediate
Test 1			
Test 2			
Test 3			
Test 4			
Total			
Comments			

Self-awareness	Most EI	Least EI	Intermediate
Test 1			
Test 2			
Test 3			
Test 4			
Test 5			
Test 6			
Total			
Comments			

Motivation	Most EI	Least EI	Intermediate
Test 1			
Test 2			
Test 3			
Test 4			
Total			
Comments			

Empathy	Most EI	Least EI	Intermediate
Test 1			
Test 2			
Test 3			
Test 4			
Total			
Comments			

Social skills	Most EI	Least EI	Intermediate
Test 1			
Test 2			
Test 3			
Total			
Comments			

Now use the box given below to enter your totals from all the tests to arrive at some grand totals. You can then use these to produce your EI profile.

Once you have studied the distribution of your scores, you can complete the next box, which will show your EI profile at a

	Most EI	Least EI	Intermediate
Self-regulation totals			
Self-awareness totals			
Motivation totals			
Empathy totals			
Social skills totals			
Grand totals			

glance. All you have to do is to decide from your scores whether you are high (H), middling (M) or low (L) on each of the five components of EI and then put ticks in the appropriate places. Now use the box given below to reflect on your profile.

	H	M	L
Self-regulation			
Self-awareness			
Motivation			
Empathy			
Social skills			

What does your profile tell you about your EI?

Provided that they are reliable (and that is for you to cross-check by means of feedback from other sources), high scores should be regarded as 'good news' – the more the better. But the chances are that you will have at least one low score, perhaps even more. If that happens, there is no reason to be too despondent. Take the results for what they are, but, more importantly, resolve to try to do something about their underlying causes.

Emotional intelligence

On which components of EI (arranged in order of importance) do you need to work?

Working to improve your EI

Once you have identified those aspects of EI on which you need to work, use the boxes given below to clarify your thoughts and feelings about them. There is no need to use all the boxes – just the ones that suit your purposes. However, make sure that you use your answers to all the boxed exercises you have done so far in order to clarify your thinking.

Self-regulation

If the analysis identifies this aspect of EI as being in need of further work, start by rereading Chapter 2. This will serve to remind you that we suggested the following as the key to improved self-regulation: defer judgement – curb impulses; park the problem – detach yourself; express yourself, but do it assertively, not aggressively; be flexible – go with the flow; don't force things; manage your non-verbal communications.

So, instead of saying, 'I must have it now' or 'I must get this off my chest', try thinking, 'Do I really want it now?' or 'What is the price of getting it off my chest?' Look back at the exercise called 'Do I really want it?' and review what you learnt from it. Similarly, if you are having trouble keeping your emotions under control, such as losing your temper at the slightest provocation, take another look at the exercise called 'Lost it recently?' Review what you noted earlier and make any changes you now consider to be necessary.

You might also take a look next at where you fit on the aggressive, assertive, non-assertive scale. Remember that there are no clear dividing lines between these three categories of behaviour, and that your actions may well vary from one type to another depending on the circumstances. Thus, it is worth giving some thought to the ways in which your behaviour is affected by your inner emotions in different circumstances. In so doing you might ask yourself, 'Why is it that I can be assertive in some situations but not in others?' and 'Why do I behave aggressively at times?'

Having done that, you might consider how flexible you are. For example, do you have trouble 'going with the flow'? Are you someone who has to have your own way? If so, why is that, and what are the consequences for you and for others? Finally, are you sensitive to your own body language and are you able to use it appropriately in different circumstances?

Self-regulation

On which aspects of self-regulation (arranged in order of importance) do you need to work?

How do you intend going about it?

Self-awareness

If your scores for self-awareness come out as being low, we suggest that you revisit Chapter 3. Self-awareness, you will recall, is about knowing yourself and what your emotions are telling you. Lack of self-awareness is not as easy to detect as lack of self-regulation, either for you or for other people. In reviewing your performance on the relevant tests you should bear in mind the following aspects of self-awareness that we identified: respect yourself; be positive; be true to yourself; give logic and rationality a rest; listen to others, and understand your impact on others.

A good starting point for that review is to ask yourself what you can do differently. For example, are you valuing yourself enough? Are you aware of what you are capable of doing in the first place? Are you looking to make things happen or do you believe that there's nothing you can do about things? What is your instinctive reaction to proposed changes – positive or negative?

You might then go on to ask yourself if you are behaving authentically – as you truly are? Are you behaving falsely because you think others expect you to be a certain way? In this context, take another look at what you wrote in the exercise you did called 'The real me?'. Make any changes that, on reflection, you now consider to be necessary.

That should lead you to ask yourself if you are over-emphasizing rationality and logic at the expense of imagination and creativity. If you feel you are on such a treadmill, try jumping off by setting yourself the task of accomplishing something outside your normal daily routines. You might even give some thought to the possibility of taking up new interests or starting a new hobby.

Listening to what others say, and reflecting on it, can help you to improve your self-awareness and, thereby, your understanding of the other components of your EI. This does not mean that you have to accept uncritically everything other people say, but their perspectives on your behaviour are worth listening to, not least because they will provide you with something against which to compare your own perceptions. Another good way of working on your self-awareness is to observe the behaviour of another person before asking yourself the question, 'How would I have behaved in such a situation?'

Finally, give some thought to how you impact on other people. Do they see you as deep or shallow, nice or nasty, gentle or violent, straightforward or devious? Then ask yourself why this is so. If you find that there are differences in the way people perceive you across a range of situations, you have again to question why this is the case. Is it your own lack of self-awareness that is causing you to project yourself in an inconsistent manner?

Self-awareness

On which aspects of self-awareness (arranged in order of importance) do you need to work?

How do you intend going about it?

Motivation

If you have scored low on motivation, reread Chapter 4. Remember, motivation is about summoning up and applying your drive, persistence and determination so as to achieve your goals. Hence, the key aspects of motivation are striving to improve and to achieve high standards; being committed to achieving your goals; taking the initiative and seizing opportunities, and being optimistic even in the face of adversity.

A good place to start your review is to ask if you are easily satisfied with too little. In other words, should you be 'raising the bar' by setting higher goals for yourself at work and/or in your personal life? In this context you should also reflect on what you said in the exercise called 'What I want to achieve in life'. Is there anything you would like to amend in the light of what you have learnt about your motivation since you completed the exercise? Similarly, there may be some important lessons to be gained from thinking hard about those things in your life that you 'gave up on'.

You might also ask yourself if you have a tendency to sit back and let others achieve for you. Is there more you could do to pull your weight in a team or a group? How do you feel about those people who work extremely hard to achieve their goals? What lessons can you learn from them?

Finally, when faced with a challenge, do you rise to the occasion or give up before you are beaten? If, say, you were diagnosed as having a serious illness, would you say, 'That's it, then, I'm a goner' or would you say, 'I'm not giving in to this. I'm going to fight it'?

Motivation

On which aspects of motivation (arranged in order of importance) do you need to work?

How do you intend going about it?

Empathy

If you scored low on empathy, reread Chapter 5. Empathy, remember, is about recognizing and reading emotions in others – specifically, being sensitive towards and understanding other people; making the needs and interests of others your point of reference; furthering the development of other people, and being tuned in, socially and politically.

As far as you are concerned, are other people's feelings there to be 'read', or are they a 'closed book', the contents of which you would rather not know about? Similarly, do you always try to appreciate other people's points of view? When dealing with others do you tacitly assume that you share the same perspectives?

You might also ask yourself how much do you 'reach out' to other people? That does not mean that you have to be actively helping them – you don't even have to like them particularly – but do you connect in small ways with people in your day-to-day interactions with them? Alternatively, are you more concerned with 'number one'? In this connection, have another look at how you responded to the exercise called 'Self-centred?'. Is there anything you would like to amend in the light of what you have learnt about yourself since you first completed this exercise?

Finally, can you take the 'emotional temperature' of a group? For example, can you sense where the power lies, and 'read' its emotional undercurrents? Similarly, are you able to enter an unfamiliar environment and work out how to become assimilated into it?

Empathy

On which aspects of empathy (arranged in order of importance) do you need to work?

How do you intend going about it?

Social skills

If your social skills are low, reread Chapter 6. You will recall that social skills are about relating to and influencing others – specifically, developing and sustaining personal relationships; and communicating with, and working with others.

With regard to the first aspect of social skills, do you still want to make new friends – or have you given up trying to do that? 'Out of sight, out of mind', it is said. Do you work at your personal relationships or do you just let them drift, relying on others to be as laissez-faire on this matter as you are?

Communicating with others is often treated as an 'optional extra', as if the consequences of not communicating do not matter. But of course you should appreciate by now that they do. So, are you someone who prefers to communicate on a 'need to know' basis, which is just one step from not communicating at all? Alternatively, are you someone who is willing to share with others what you know and how you feel?

Finally, are you a team player, a person who can work in a team for some of the time at least, or simply an individualist who is only interested in yourself? In this context, take another look at how you responded to the exercise called 'Team player'. Is there anything you would like to amend in the light of what you have learnt about yourself since you first completed this exercise? For example, are you able to work with others without anxiety and discomfort, or are there times when the strain is too much for you?

Social skills

On which aspects of social skills (arranged in order of importance) do you need to work?

How do you intend going about it?

Commercially available products for testing your EI

The tests we have given you were put together especially for this book. They will have given you a reading of your EI. You will also have gained some insight from your answers to the assorted questions in Chapter 1. However, if you wish to compare the insights you have gained form this book with what will be revealed by other means, here are some inventories available from commercial sources:

- EQ-I, developed by Reuven Bar-On for his consultancy Pro-Philes, available from Multi-Health Systems Inc; offices in Toronto and New York State.
- Emotional Intelligence Questionnaire, developed by Malcolm Higgs and Victor Dulewicz, available from ASE.
- OPQ32 EI, available from Saville & Holdsworth Ltd.
- WPQei, available from The Test Agency.
- Emotional Competence Inventory (ECI), developed by Daniel Goleman, Richard Boyatzis and the HayGroup, available from HayMcBer.
- MEIS Emotional IQ Test, developed by John Mayer, Peter Salovey and David Caruso (availability unknown).

There is a short test of EI in Chapter 9 of *IQ May Get You a Job: EQ gets you promoted* by Gilles Azzopardi (Foulsham, 2001).

Online testing of EI is currently available from at least the E-Mode and Queendom Web sites. It will be worth your while to surf the Web from time to time to see if something new is on offer. Our advice is to do these tests in the same spirit as you have done the tests in this book, and to subject the outcomes to the same rigorous process of analysis and reflection.

Looking forward

Once maturity has arrived, no one expects to become intellec-
tually more able – though experience can help us to use our
innate mental abilities more effectively. The same is true of EI.
If you are prepared to derive lessons from your experience,
and those of other people, you can learn a great deal that will
be of benefit to you: for example, when and how to count to
10; go with the flow; listen actively; give your brain a rest;
prepare yourself emotionally for the big occasion; read the
emotional landscape, and become more subtle in the way you
deal with others – and yourself. In other words, you can learn
to marshal your inner feelings so as to become a better person.
By 'better' we mean what we said at the beginning: being a
person who is capable of using the relevant skills constructively in order to make your day-to-day dealings with others
more positive, pleasant and productive. In the process, there is
every chance that you will become a more rounded and self-
fulfilled person.

If you intend to work on developing your EI – and that is
something we can all do – then you should recognize that it may
be some time before the benefits identified above begin to
accrue. After all, you may be seeking to change habits that have
been a long time in the making! Consequently, we suggest that it
is worth letting a few months elapse before using some of the
commercially available products listed above for testing your
EI. Similarly, there is nothing to stop you at that stage from
working through the test items provided in this book again. If,
as we recommended, you made a careful note of how you
performed the first time of asking, you should be able to see
whether or not there are any significant improvements.
However, if you have been giving some serious thought to the
development of your EI and in the process monitored your own
progress, you will probably have a strong sense of where you
have got to without having to answer the questions.

Postscript

Should there be improvement? Is it mistaken to endorse a model of emotional development that places the emphasis solely on the positive? There are certainly other positions. For example, Dr Carl Rogers, the US psychologist (acknowledged by many to be the founder of the human potential movement), said of his own life experiences that he would 'like to treasure the feelings of anger and tenderness and shame and hurt and love and anxiety and giving and fear – all the positive and negative reactions that crop up'. To him, both negative and positive emotions were an enriching part of his existence. This idea is further developed in an intriguingly titled book *The Psychology of Man's Possible Evolution*, by the Russian philosopher and mystic P D Ouspensky, in which he wrote, 'What would happen to all our life, without negative emotions? What would happen to what we call art, to the theatre, to drama, to most novels?'

Actually, there is no danger of negative emotion going away because there is too much of it in most people's lives for that – just think of all that envy, greed and hatred. Negative emotions, however, are corrosive and ultimately destructive, to self and to others. But where does that leave art and artists? We don't want to lose them. Ouspensky's remark is reminiscent of something Freud said, that all art stems from neurotic behaviour, which of course stems from negative emotions. However, not all artists are neurotics, nor, of course, are all neurotics artists – there are far too many of them for that. So, let us not suppose that by suppressing negative emotion (even if this were possible), art and artists will go to the wall. In fact, artists ought to be able to thrive on all shades of emotion – after all, Shakespeare wrote both *Macbeth* and *A Midsummer Night's Dream*. Artists themselves often distinguish between their 'dark' and 'sunny' creations. The point is that artists have EI like anyone else, so why should they not benefit from exercising it? Creativity's 'ugly sister' is what Irving Welsh, author of *Trainspotting*, calls discipline. If we put that in terms of EI, artists might appreciate that creativity (self-awareness) needs discipline (self-regulation and motivation) if it is to flourish. As for the rest of us, if we tapped more often into our creativity – gave the brain a rest – there might be more artists and more artistic endeavour.

Negative emotions do not need to be encouraged; there are enough people in the world whose behaviour provides evidence of that. Why not say – unconditionally – that all of us, both those who are not artists and those who are, benefit from displacing negative with positive emotion? Any reduction at all in the amount of negative emotion in all our lives is worth having.

Further reading from Kogan Page

Other titles in the Testing series

Career, Aptitude and Selection Tests, Jim Barrett, 1998

How to Master Personality Questionnaires, 2nd edn, Mark Parkinson, 2000

How to Master Psychometric Tests, 2nd edn, Mark Parkinson, 2000

How to Pass Advanced Aptitude Tests, Jim Barrett, 2002

How to Pass at an Assessment Centre, Harry Tolley and Bob Wood, 2001

How to Pass Computer Selection Tests, Sanjay Modha, 1994

How to Pass Graduate Psychometric Tests, 2nd edn, Mike Bryon, 2001

How to Pass Numeracy Tests, 2nd edn, Harry Tolley and Ken Thomas, 2000

How to Pass Professional-level Psychometric Tests, Sam Al-Jajjoka, 2001

How to Pass Selection Tests, 2nd edn, Mike Bryon and Sanjay Modha, 1998

How to Pass Technical Selection Tests, Mike Bryon and Sanjay Modha, 1993

How to Pass the Civil Service Qualifying Tests, Mike Bryon, 1995

How to Pass the Police Initial Recruitment Test, Harry Tolley, Ken Thomas and Catherine Tolley, 1997

How to Pass Verbal Reasoning Tests, Harry Tolley and Ken Thomas, 2000

Rate Yourself!, Marthe Sansregret and Dyane Adams, 1998

Test Your IQ, Ken Russell and Philip Carter, 2000

Test Your Own Aptitude, 2nd edn, Jim Barrett and Geoff Williams, 1990

Test Yourself!, Jim Barrett, 2000

The Times Book of IQ Tests – Book Two, Ken Russell and Philip Carter, 2002

The Times Book of IQ Tests – Book One, Ken Russell and Philip Carter, 2001

Also available on CD ROM in association with *The Times*

Published by Kogan Page Interactive, *The Times* Testing series is an exciting new range of interactive CD ROMs that will provide invaluable, practice tests for both job applicants and for those seeking a brain-stretching challenge. Each CD ROM features:

- over 1,000 unique interactive questions;
- instant scoring with feedback and analysis;
- hours of practice with randomly generated test;
- questions devised by top UK MENSA puzzles editors and test experts;
- against-the-clock, real test conditions.

Current titles available:
Brain Teasers Volume 1, 2002
Psychometric Tests Volume 1, 2002
Test Your IQ Volume 1, 2002
Test Your Aptitude Volume 1, 2002

Interview and career guidance

The A–Z of Careers and Jobs, 10th edn, Irene Krechowiecka, 2002

Act Your Way Into a New Job, Deb Gottesman and Buzz Mauro, 1999

Changing Your Career, Sally Longson, 2000

Choosing Your Career, Simon Kent, 1997

Creating Your Career, Simon Kent, 1997

From CV to Shortlist, Tony Vickers, 1997

Graduate Job Hunting Guide, Mark Parkinson, 2001

Great Answers to Tough Interview Questions, 5th edn, Martin John Yate, 2001

How You Can Get That Job!, 3rd edn, Rebecca Corfield, 2002

The Job-Hunter's Handbook, 2nd edn, David Greenwood, 1999

Job-Hunting Made Easy, 3rd edn, John Bramham and David Cox, 1995

Landing Your First Job, Andrea Shavick, 1999

Net That Job!, 2nd edn, Irene Krechowiecka, 2000

Odd Jobs, 2nd edn, Simon Kent, 2002

Offbeat Careers, 3rd edn, Vivien Donald, 1995

Online Job-Hunting: Great Answers to Tough Interview Questions, Martin John Yate and Terra Dourlain, 2001

Preparing Your Own CV, 3rd edn, Rebecca Corfield, 2002

Readymade CVs, 2nd edn, Lynn Williams, 2000
Readymade Job Search Letters, 2nd edn, Lynn Williams, 2000
Successful Interview Skills, 3rd edn, Rebecca Corfield, 2002
Your Job Search Made Easy, 3rd edn, Mark Parkinson, 2002

Further advice on a variety of specific career paths can also be found in Kogan Page's *Careers in...* series and *Getting a Top Job in...* series. Please visit the Web site at the address below for more details.

The above titles are available from all good bookshops. For further information, please contact the publisher at the following address:

Kogan Page Limited
120 Pentonville Road
London N1 9JN
UK
Tel: 020 7278 0433
Fax: 020 7837 6348
www.kogan-page.co.uk